# Mysterious Bones
## The Story of Kennewick Man

*by* KATHERINE KIRKPATRICK

*illustrated by*

EMMA STEVENSON

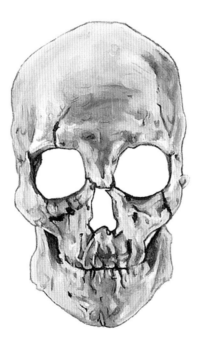

Holiday House / New York

In honor of the Ancient One,
Kennewick Man
K. K.

To Gary
with all my love
E. S.

Text copyright © 2011 by Katherine Kirkpatrick
Illustrations copyright © 2011 by Emma Stevenson
All Rights Reserved
HOLIDAY HOUSE is registered in the U.S. Patent and Trademark Office.
The text typeface is Breughel.
The artwork for this book was created
with gouache on watercolor paper.
Printed and bound in March 2011 at Tien Wah Press,
Johor Bahru, Johor, Malaysia.
www.holidayhouse.com
First Edition
1   3   5   7   9   10   8   6   4   2

Library of Congress Cataloging-in-Publication Data
Kirkpatrick, Katherine.
Mysterious bones : the story of Kennewick Man / by Katherine Kirkpatrick ;
illustrated by Emma Stevenson. — 1st ed.
p. cm.
ISBN 978-0-8234-2187-9 (hardcover)
1. Kennewick Man—Juvenile literature. 2. Human remains (Archaeology)—
Repatriation—Washington (State)—Juvenile literature. 3. Cultural property—
Repatriation—United States—Juvenile literature. 4. Indians of North America—
Origin—Juvenile literature. 5. Indians of North America—Washington (State)—
Antiquities—Juvenile literature. 6. Washington (State)—Antiquities—Juvenile
literature. I. Stevenson, Emma, ill. II. Title.
E78.W3K57 2011
979.7'01—dc22
2009025575

## Author's Note

In this book, I try to offer as many different viewpoints as possible. I introduce topics in sidebars that are as important as what's discussed in the main text. Readers may find what appear to be contradictions. I want to show that there are no hard-and-fast answers for a subject as multifaceted as Kennewick Man/the Ancient One.

Above all, I hope this book will stimulate discussion. It is through discussion that we can come to mutual understandings and solutions for many of life's problems and, ultimately, bring healing to our planet.

# Contents

*Kennewick Man's discovery site, Columbia Park, Washington*

# Discovery

The piercing roar of hydroplanes split the air over the shallow, muddy river. Will Thomas and his seven college buddies pushed through the crowd in the parking area of Columbia Park in Kennewick, Washington, and headed for the ticket gate. Beyond it, the long riverbank was packed with spectators.

It was Sunday afternoon, July 28, 1996, the last day of the Water Follies, an annual weekend of sports events. Will and his friends had arrived too late to get good seats for the speedboat races, and they wondered whether the event was worth the $11 admission fee. It was 108 degrees—scorching hot even for a summer's day on the sunburnt grasslands of the Tri-Cities of southeastern Washington State: Kennewick, Richland, and Pasco.

The young men talked the matter over. Someone suggested crashing the gate. They could enter the race area through the brush beyond the park entrance. Deciding to give it a try, the group moved from the parking lot to a thicket of grasses and bushes, trees and reeds. Their sneakers sank in the mud, and thorny plants pricked their bare legs. After about ten minutes, one of them said, "I've had enough of this," and everyone except Will and his friend Dave Deacy headed back to the gate to pay the fee. The two of them pressed on toward the Columbia River.

Sloshing through the knee-high water, Will found, was easier than battling the mud and waist-high marsh grass. Dave chose to walk along the bank, even if it meant having to duck his head to avoid tree branches. Both ways were slow going.

Will didn't kick up too much mud, and the river was calm enough that he could see the bottom. Near a clump of grass jutting above the water, he spotted something tan and round. "Look over here, dude!" he called. "We have a human head!"

"Get out!" Dave replied.

"No, really, man—it's a head! There's a dead body here! Someone's been murdered!"

Will freed the object from the mud and lifted it in his hands. It *was* a human skull. Or the top half of one. Mud dripped from the eye sockets. The upper jaw held a row of worn yellowed teeth.

"Put it back in the water!" Dave urged.

"No," Will said. "We should go to the police." Then he realized that reporting the discovery would hold them up and they'd miss the Follies. Will decided he'd hide the skull, go to the races, and *then* report what they had found to the police. He placed the skull in a low-growing bush near the water.

Several hours later, after the last hydroplane race had been run and everyone was leaving, Will told his friends about the skull. The other boys didn't believe him. Just the same, one of them got an empty paint bucket from his truck. If Will was going to fetch the skull, he'd need something to carry it in.

While the others waited, Will and Dave retraced their path through the thicket toward the bush beside the river. The skeleton head was still there. When they returned to the parking area, the guys stood in a circle and gaped at the muddy skull.

Thomas had seen plenty of police officers around the park earlier in the day, directing traffic and keeping the crowds in line. Across the parking lot, he now spotted a man in a blue uniform. He flagged the policeman and, bucket in hand, walked toward him.

A short time later, the policeman delivered the skull to the local coroner's office. Because the skull was yellow with age, the coroner, Floyd Johnson, realized it wasn't a recent death. He assigned James (Jim) Chatters, a local archaeologist with his own consulting firm, to investigate the case. Right away, Chatters, police officers, and search-and-rescue personnel traveled by police boat to the location where the skull had been found. The search party beamed their flashlights along the shallow bottom of the river. Piece by piece they located additional parts of a skeleton.

The next morning, under Chatters's keen inspection, the riverbank yielded even more bones. It was now Chatters's job to study them. They all appeared to be from a single skeleton, and he needed to determine as much as he could about them.

In the basement of his house in nearby Richland, Chatters carefully spread out the bones on his laboratory table. There were more than three hundred bones in all. He placed the skull at one end of the table and then arranged the other bones, many still covered with dirt, according to their place in a human body. Studying bones was like doing a puzzle, and Chatters loved a good puzzle. By carefully inspecting and measuring the bones, from the large leg and pelvic segments to the tiny joints, he'd soon be able to tell if the skeleton was of a man or a woman, how old he or she had been at death, height, general state of health, and many other details. The bones might even reveal how the person had died.

Chatters concluded that nearly every bone of the skeleton's body had been found. It's always easier to put a puzzle together, he knew, if all the pieces are there.

Chatters had a Ph.D. in anthropology from the University of Washington. He had taught on the university level and worked as a research scientist at the Pacific Northwest National Laboratory in Richland. He had had a lot of experience studying bones. He could tell at once from the shape of the hip bone that this skeleton was of a man. The sutures, or seams in the skull—which gradually mesh together as a person ages—indicated that the man had been between forty and fifty-five years old when he died. The length of a leg bone showed that he had been five feet nine inches tall. From the bones' golden color, Chatters decided they were at least a hundred years old.

At first, Chatters thought that the man had been a pioneer. Near the bones in the river, he had found a rusty knife with a bone handle of a style popular in the late 1800s. And the long, narrow shape of the man's skull suggested to Chatters that the man was of European ancestry.

But in another respect the skeleton didn't seem European at all. Though the man hadn't lost a single tooth and didn't have any cavities, his teeth were ground down. That meant he'd eaten food with sand in it, such as tough meat, gritty fish, roots, and plants. Teeth like this usually were found in the remains of Native Americans who'd lived hundreds of years ago.

Determining the skeleton's race was important. According to law, if the bones proved to be those of a

Native American, they could be claimed by a tribe with shared ancestry. This law was called the Native American Graves Protection and Repatriation Act (NAGPRA).

In fact, the Confederated Tribes of the Umatilla Indian Reservation had already been told of the skeleton's discovery and were awaiting a formal decision of custodianship. It was the U.S. Army Corps of Engineers, an agency of the federal government, that had legal custody, since the Corps owned Columbia Park, where the skeleton had been found. It was the Corps' responsibility to keep the tribes informed.

The Confederated Tribes, made up of the Umatilla, Walla Walla, and Cayuse peoples, had lived in the Kennewick area but had been moved by the U.S. government in 1855 to a reservation in Oregon seventy-five miles away. If the remains were Native American, the Umatilla wanted to return the bones to the earth just as soon as they could take custody of them.

Chatters's scientific training had taught him that it was important to gather as much information as possible before coming to a conclusion. Carefully examining one bone at a time, he continued his work.

Broken ribs on both sides of the body showed that the man had suffered a violent blow or collision. He'd survived the trauma, and his bones had partially healed. Perhaps he'd been struck by a large animal, like a bison, or endured the kick of an elk. Or he could have fallen down a hill or off a cliff.

Next Chatters studied the man's arm bones. His right shoulder showed a small fracture in the socket that had occurred near the time of his death and had only partially healed.

The bone of the right arm was larger and more massive than that of his left arm. In life, the man's right arm must have been amazingly robust. He'd clearly been right-handed. A person's bones change size and shape according to how the bones are used, and certain activities can add mass to bones. The man had powerful shoulder and arm muscles, probably from a lifetime of hunting.

As the man aged, he may have suffered arthritis, or joint disease, which meant he would have felt pain in his knees and elbows, his lower back, and especially his neck.

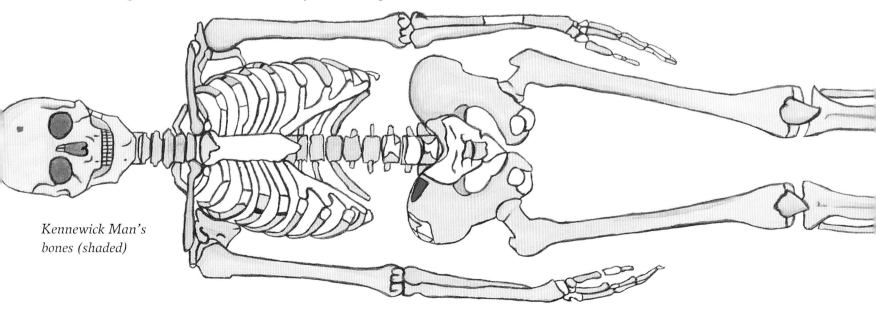

*Kennewick Man's bones (shaded)*

A dime-sized dent on the left side of his forehead showed another injury. Here, as in other parts of the skeleton, the bone had healed. More questions arose. Had the man been struck? Or was he hurt accidentally?

Chatters paused from reading his notes. For the first time, he took a close look at the skeleton's pelvis. He realized there was something out of the ordinary about it. A dirty rocklike object was embedded in the bone. With the utmost care, he reached to touch the object.

Until now, Chatters had thought that the man had been Caucasian—say, a fur trapper or a pioneer. However, when he examined the pelvis carefully, his mind raced ahead to the astonishing possibility that the object, which was made of volcanic rock, might be a Cascade point, a kind of spear point that hunter-gatherers had used in the central Washington area thousands of years ago. If the object turned out to be a Cascade point, it would indicate the skeleton was not from the 1800s but was at least 5,000 years old—and maybe as much as 9,000 years old. Few complete skeletons from that period had ever been found.

Chatters couldn't wait to get a better look at the object, and he soon had the chance. The staff at the local hospital occasionally performed jobs for the coroner's office after their X-ray work with patients was finished for the day. At the hospital that evening, July 29, Chatters watched an X-ray machine reveal a blurry, oval shape within the pelvic bone. Unfortunately, the image that emerged wasn't clear enough to show any details. And since it was the lab's closing time, there wouldn't be any more X-rays taken that night.

The following evening, Chatters returned to the hospital. This time, a technician would make a three-dimensional CT (computerized tomography) scan of the bone, a test superior to an X-ray. The results were very satisfactory.

Chatters caught his breath as a slender leaf shape, a little more than 2 inches (5 centimeters) long and 0.8 inch (2 centimeters) wide, came into focus. It *was* a projectile point! The rounded base showed that it was a spear point rather than an arrow point—used by later people—because it had a wide base for fitting into a thick shaft. Its tip had broken off, but the remaining razor-sharp edge had cut into the pelvic bone. The point was so deeply embedded in the pelvis that the person who launched it must have used an *atlatl*, or throwing stick.

Bone around the point indicated healing: The man had survived the assault long enough for the bone to regrow. But a crescent-shaped area around it showed an infection. The man had probably lived with a painful, open, smelly sore for months or even years. Perhaps, over time, it was this infection that had killed him.

The spear point was an exciting discovery. It meant that the skeleton was much too old to have been a pioneer. But who was he? Many puzzling questions remained about the skeleton's ancestry and how long ago he'd died.

In the next few days, Chatters showed the skeleton to several local colleagues who were specialists in human bones. These anthropologists were baffled. The shape of the skull, showing a narrow, projecting face, indicated to them that the individual might have been of European ancestry. How could an apparently European skeleton have a projectile point, crafted in a prehistoric style, lodged in its hip? As nearly all the world believed, "white" people hadn't existed thousands of years ago in America.

According to popular theory, the first Americans, also known as Paleoindians, looked like many Asians, with broad faces. By this time in 1996, a few scholarly articles had been published suggesting that skulls of ancient

## *Why Study Skeletons?*

By studying a human skeleton, people can learn how bodies are constructed and how they work. Medical students study bones, as well as muscles and organs, so as doctors they can help people recover from accidents and illnesses.

Physical anthropologists are scientists who study human anatomy. By examining a skeleton, they can determine the person's age, sex, how long ago he or she died, whether the person had injuries or diseases, and, in a general way, what the person looked like. They can sometimes tell the cause of death, whether a weapon was used, and, if so, what kind of weapon. Physical anthropologists help police with the identification of crime victims.

Paleoanthropologists specialize in the origins and anatomy of early humans and try to answer such questions as how having two legs and standing upright helped early humans succeed as a species. Other anthropologists study how the peoples of the world over millions of years developed different body types in order to adapt to their specialized ways of life. Through such studies, we can learn much about the history of humankind.

Paleoindian skeletons were shaped differently from those of modern-day Native Americans. But this information was not widely known. To the anthropologists looking at the skeleton with Chatters, the age of the bones was a mystery.

Laboratory tests might provide more answers. Chatters knew that the most accurate test for determining the age of anything, including a skeleton, is radiocarbon dating. All plant and animal matter contain traces of the element carbon, which includes a radioactive form that starts to decay when the plant or animal dies. It would be possible to date the skeleton by determining how much radioactive carbon it contained. But radiocarbon dating would require sending a small piece of bone to a laboratory—and the test itself would destroy the bone.

Chatters thought about the Native Americans who were interested in claiming the skeleton. Though Native Americans come from many traditions, most if not all tribes believe that a deceased person should go into the next world with all body parts intact.

One evening while Chatters struggled in his laboratory with the question of how to proceed, his wife, Jenny Elf, stopped by. As he stared at the skeleton in its protective plastic bags, Jenny asked, "So how's Kennewick Man?"

Now the skeleton had a name.

Chatters explained his dilemma about the testing. Elf, who is part Haida, a Native American tribe from the area that is now Alaska and British Columbia, said she'd be in favor of the radiocarbon analysis. "If it's an ancient Indian," she said, "that makes him my ancestor, and I want to know how old he is." Chatters suddenly wondered if Kennewick Man could be related to their daughter, Claire. He hadn't considered that intriguing idea before.

He made phone calls to discuss the possibility of laboratory analysis with the coroner and with an archaeologist with the Army Corps of Engineers. Later there would be a question of whether the correct procedures had been followed, especially in regard to the Corps not consulting with the Umatilla. Chatters decided to request the testing.

Chatters selected a tiny bone connecting one of Kennewick Man's pinky fingers to the rest of his hand. He sent it to a laboratory at the University of California, Riverside. At the same time, he arranged for a lab at the University of California, Davis, to receive the remaining bone fragment after the first lab was finished sampling it. The second lab would conduct DNA testing on the remaining part of the bone. While radiocarbon testing is best for revealing a skeleton's age, DNA testing, which analyzes genetic material, reveals more about a person's makeup and thus provides information about his or her ancestors.

Three weeks went by. Chatters waited anxiously for the test results. Finally, the two laboratories called him. The DNA test had proved inconclusive. But the radiocarbon test had yielded a date. The voice on the other end of the phone indicated from her tone that Chatters might be in for a surprise. She asked him, "Are you sitting down?" The caller told Chatters that Kennewick Man had lived . . . approximately 9,500 years ago!

Chatters gave a shout of celebration, then sat down in stunned silence. He could hardly believe the news. Kennewick Man was among the oldest skeletons ever found in the Americas. And only eight of them had skulls as complete as Kennewick Man's. For twenty years, Chatters had been studying eastern Washington State prehistory from remains such as stone tools. For the first time, he'd have the opportunity to glimpse prehistory by studying a well-preserved skeleton.

# Controversy

TV lights were blindingly bright inside the windowless room of Kennewick City Hall. Cameras flashed. The date was Tuesday, August 27, 1996. It had been a month since Kennewick Man had washed out of the bank of the Columbia River.

Jim Chatters, in his usual flannel shirt and jeans, joined Kennewick's mayor and coroner at a table for a press conference. Journalists, city officials, and other curious onlookers from the small agricultural community formed the assemblage.

Coroner Floyd Johnson told about the skeleton's discovery and described the radiocarbon dating, then opened the floor to questions. Most reporters directed their questions to Chatters.

"What's a European doing here nine thousand years ago?" a TV reporter asked.

Chatters's use of the phrase "Caucasoid in appearance" had confused his listeners, who understood the information to mean the skeleton was of a "white" person.

"We're not saying this *is* a European," Chatters said. He then explained that Kennewick Man did share certain characteristics, in his skull and leg bones, that are found in Europeans today.

"Where do you think he came from?" another reporter asked.

"He was probably from this region," Chatters said. "I suspect he was probably even born within one to two hundred miles of where he died."

"If he's been there nine thousand years, why wasn't he found before?"

"We had that severe flooding last February, and I think it was that event that washed his remains out of the riverbank." Chatters went on to explain how calcium in the soil, gradually seeping into the skeleton's bones, had kept Kennewick Man from rotting away.

Through Chatters's detailed answers, the audience started to think about the skeleton more and more as a human being. Chatters said he admired this man who'd lived with so many injuries and pains and who had survived at least one violent assault. Everything he knew about Kennewick Man revealed him to be a tenacious survivor.

"What happened to his people?" someone asked. "Did they die out?"

"We don't know. Possibly. But given the thousands of years ago that he lived, and assuming he had any children of his own, he probably could be considered ancestral to all modern American Indians. . . ." He paused. "In fact," he continued, "given the four hundred fifty or so generations since he died, he is probably an ancestor of everyone."

There were murmurs as people took in this information. Then someone asked if Kennewick Man would go on display at a museum anytime soon.

"No," Chatters answered. He declined to show the slides that the coroner had brought to the press conference. He knew that displaying pictures of a skeleton would surely anger many Native Americans because of their

## What Is Race?

"Race does not exist. Racism does exist."
                        —Charles Keyes, anthropologist

"Race" is a general term used as a basis for dividing human groups into categories. It is a social concept; it describes how individuals see each other in society.

Numerous overlapping physical characteristics exist among people of different heritages, or ethnicities. Characteristics such as tallness and shortness, dark skin and light skin, curly hair and straight hair are not always predictable signs of a person's country of origin. This is why "race" is not an accurate term for describing how people are biologically different from one another.

People can be divided into geographical groups according to the locations where they or their ancestors came from. They can be divided according to the customs they follow or their native language. They can be grouped according to their physical characteristics, known as traits; or by blood type; or by very specific genetic information carried in their DNA.

The word "race" tends to combine these separate areas of biology, geography, and customs when classifying people. And though the term is neither precise nor accurate, it continues to be used when someone wants to form a judgment quickly.

In the 1800s, anthropologists studied, as they do today, the shapes of skulls and other features to help them determine a person's "race" or "ethnicity." The physical differences suggested three distinct races: "Negroid" (black or African), "Caucasoid" (European or white), and "Mongoloid" (Asian and Native American). Today specialists acknowledge that determining race is a far more complex issue—that individuals have many hundreds of traits and are often difficult to categorize. Scientists still use physical features and skull shapes as guidelines, but increasingly, they rely on blood types and on DNA analysis—the study of genetic material—to determine a person's ancestry.

Anthropologists now know that, over time, physical differences between people have evolved. (*See* "Why Study Skeletons?" sidebar.) Modern peoples often look very different from their ancestors. Even by carefully studying Kennewick Man's skull shape, physical anthropologists cannot place him in any modern-day racial or ethnic category—a subject that has caused much confusion and debate.

The word "race" continues to change in meaning. Each time there is a U.S. Census, there is a slightly different list of categories under the heading of *Race*. The 2000 Census included seven categories, while the 2010 Census included fifteen categories.

belief that the dead man's spirit could be captured in those photos. At the very least, such public display would be considered disrespectful and in poor taste. And the legal matter of the skeleton's custody had not yet been resolved.

The media event concluded with a reporter asking the coroner, "What was your reaction when you found out how old the skeleton was?"

"I was astounded," the coroner answered.

Another reporter chimed in. "What about you, Dr. Chatters?"

"Well," Chatters replied, "it's like I've been following this man's tracks my whole life, studying the things he left behind: campsites, dwellings, trash piles. I thought I knew who I was following—what he looked like. But when I finally caught up with him and he turned around . . . he wasn't who I expected to see."

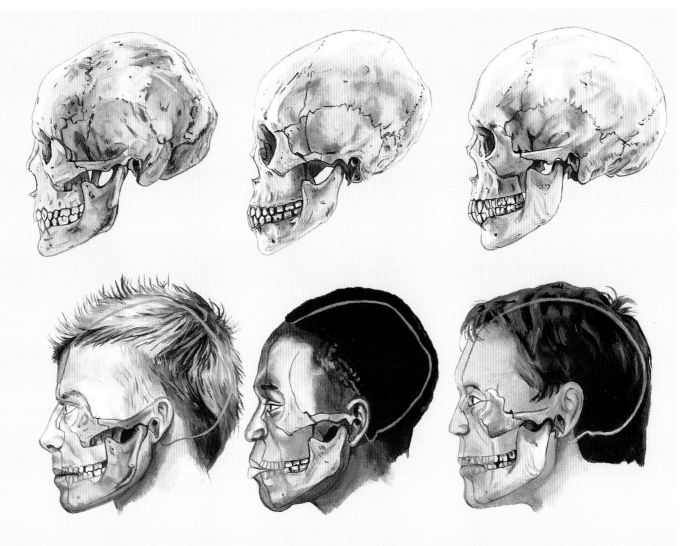

*The three skull shapes, representing the three major races of the world—a concept devised in the 1800s—is now considered simplistic and out of date. However, skull measurements can still be useful in determining a person's ancestry. When comparing skulls, physical anthropologists look at indicators such as a roundness or elongation of skull; projection or flatness of facial region including prominence of cheekbones; height of the face; form of the chin; and differences in teeth.*

Less than an hour later, the story was being broadcast on several national TV news programs. Suddenly, millions of viewers knew about Kennewick Man.

At the same time, news of the skeleton's age reached the Confederated Tribes of the Umatilla Indian Reservation in Pendleton, Oregon. The board of trustees discussed the matter. In its view, the sacred remains of an ancestor had been desecrated through the radiocarbon testing and the DNA analysis. The board arranged a meeting with the Army Corps of Engineers, the skeleton's legal custodian.

The next morning was as sweltering as the day Kennewick Man had been discovered. The Umatilla had chosen the site where the skeleton had been found as the place to confer with four Corps members as well as Chatters. Altogether, twelve men gathered, including members of a neighboring tribe, the Wanapum Band, who'd been invited by Umatilla leaders.

On a strip of sun-bleached lawn near the Columbia River, the Umatilla expressed their disapproval of both the testing and the press conference. Armand Minthorn, a board member and the principal religious leader of the Umatilla, requested that no more studies be made of the skeleton. He also asked that there be no more publicity. But the controversy had already spread far beyond the arid plateau of eastern Washington.

In the following days, Umatilla elders named the skeleton *Oid-p'ma Natitayt*, in the native tongue of Sahaptin, or the Ancient One. Umatilla custom discourages talking about the dead in public, but Minthorn soon took on the role as spokesperson for the Confederated Tribes. Eventually, he regarded the publicity as an opportunity to educate people about Native Americans. "Our old people say that once a body goes in the ground, it must stay in the ground. Our teachings say the dead must be buried. Their presence in the soil makes the land sacred."

Chatters expressed an entirely different point of view. "Kennewick Man is too old to be considered the ancestor of any modern group," he said. "This was a man who spoke a language now dead, lived in a culture long forgotten, among a people who no longer exist. We owe it to him and his people to give them a proper place in human history, not shove knowledge of them aside for the sake of temporal political expediency. . . . Reburial without study is forever."

# An Ancestor or a "Find"?

In the 1800s and early 1900s, government officials and American soldiers regularly dug up Native American graves. Some bodies were decapitated because the surgeon general of the United States wanted the skulls for study.

From 1906 to as late as 1972, the U.S. government would pass a series of laws that prohibited looting and regulated the collecting and handling of Native American remains by archaeologists. From the Native American perspective, the carting off of bones and grave objects to museums and universities by archaeologists—regardless of legality or purpose—was grave robbing and a violation of basic human rights. Meanwhile, the illegal looting of Indian graves by artifact collectors continued.

On the Columbia Plateau, mostly in the 1940s and 1950s, and continuing in the 1960s and 1970s, the Army Corps of Engineers removed many Native American graves when dams were being built on the Columbia River. Archaeologists working for the government dug up Native American cemeteries to preserve them from flooding. Sometimes instead of reburying the dead, the archaeologists placed the bones in museums where they'd remain indefinitely in storage (until after 1990 when NAGPRA was passed, *see* "What Is NAGPRA?" sidebar).

When Kennewick Man surfaced from the Columbia River bank in 1996, there were still many elderly Plateau Tribal members living who'd witnessed these activities during the dam-building era. In a few cases, they'd seen archaeologists dig up the graves of their own parents and grandparents.

Few members of the general public would comprehend or sympathize with Native Americans who later would draw comparisons between the government's handling of an ancient skeleton to the desecration of recent ancestors. To the Umatilla and other Plateau tribes, such a connection was both obvious and heartfelt.

In the view of the Umatilla, the scientific study of the Ancient One, against the tribes' expressed disapproval, amounted to yet another human-rights violation.

The same day as the press conference at Kennewick City Hall, Chatters had placed a call to Doug Owsley of the Smithsonian Institution in Washington, D.C. The well-known physical anthropologist expressed a keen interest in seeing Kennewick Man. He asked if Chatters would be willing to fly to Washington, D.C., with the skeleton. The two-day trip would be paid for by Owsley's grant money. A plan temporarily to take the Ancient One to Washington, D.C., formed as both Chatters and the Umatilla consulted with attorneys.

On Friday, August 30, three days after the press conference, coroner Floyd Johnson came and got the skeleton from Chatters. Chatters had not yet completed his official report to the coroner. But there was now the question of whether the law was being followed. The Washington, D.C., trip would have to be canceled.

## What Is NAGPRA?

On November 16, 1990, President George H. W. Bush signed into law the Native American Graves Protection and Repatriation Act (NAGPRA). The law protects the graves of Native Americans from being disturbed. It also provides rights to Native Americans to ensure that the remains of their ancestors, along with associated burial objects, cannot be owned as property by museums or government agencies without permission. Previous laws had already provided these protections to the rest of the United States citizens.

NAGPRA is a human-rights law designed to address the widespread destruction of Indian graves—a practice that has occurred and continues today when looters sell human remains and burial goods to collectors. Massive numbers of Native American dead—over a million individuals—have been dug up in the United States. In the 1800s and up until the mid-1900s, it was common practice by soldiers, government agents, professional and amateur archaeologists, and others to dig up human remains and place them in museums.

Because of the tremendously large number of Native American grave thefts, it is taking years for the stolen or improperly acquired human remains to be returned to the appropriate tribes. As of May 17, 2010, new regulations became effective that provide direction on how to repatriate Culturally Unidentified Individuals (CUI). NAGPRA's Review Committee, made up of tribal leaders, museum professionals, and anthropologists, monitors the repatriation process and makes recommendations in cases where there are CUIs, non-federally recognized tribes, and competing claims.

NAGPRA has been the focus of much debate among lawyers, tribes, museum curators, scientists, and others. Some scientists feel that the act is overly restrictive in terms of providing access to—and thus scientific study of—human remains, especially ancient ones. On the other hand, some Native Americans feel that NAGPRA should be amended to include additional restrictions relating to the treatment and possession of the ancient dead.

Reluctantly, Chatters handed over the large plywood box he'd built for Kennewick Man. He'd wrapped each bone individually in a plastic bag and had carefully assembled them in the box, packing the largest ones first. One by one, he added the rest of the bones.

The bones were taken to the sheriff's office in Kennewick. Two days later, the Army Corps of Engineers moved them to nearby Richland, to the Battelle-Richland facility, a large office building where the Corps rented a suite of rooms. Meanwhile, the Ancient One's age continued to make newspaper headlines, and soon articles were appearing in national magazines like *Time* and *Newsweek*.

As events unfolded, Umatilla leaders knew that repatriating—reclaiming and being responsible for—the skeleton would be no simple matter. It would be difficult for them to demonstrate their cultural affiliation with an individual who was as much as 9,500 years old. So the Umatilla joined four other Native American groups—the Confederated Tribes of the Colville Reservation, the Nez Percé Tribe, the Confederated Tribes and Bands of the Yakama Indian Nation, and the Wanapum Band. From this point on, they would work together to repatriate the Ancient One.

All these groups had lived for thousands of years in the Columbia River Basin, in the general geographical region of Kennewick. Their ancestral lands covered millions of acres. The Ancient One, if not an Umatilla ancestor, could have belonged to any of the other groups. Because the Columbia Plateau tribes frequently intermarried, they believed they all shared blood and thus ancestry with the Ancient One. The tribes sought to bury the skeleton immediately, except for the Colville, who favored noninvasive study before interment.

The five tribes, as a coalition, sent word to the Corps, claiming the skeleton. On September 13, 1996, the Corps responded. It promised the Ancient One to the five tribes. The Corps officially announced that, by virtue of age, the skeleton was Native American. It said that there was a shared group identity that could be reasonably traced to the tribes. "Shared group identity," according to the NAGPRA law, meant that the coalition shared a cultural affiliation with Kennewick Man's people—in this case, based on a common geographical area. The Corps set a date of October 23, 1996, to hand the remains over to tribal representatives.

Armand Minthorn, the Umatilla religious leader, selected a secret burial spot for the Ancient One and planned for the reburial to take place the day after the tribes gained custody.

Meanwhile, across the continent in Washington, D.C., Doug Owsley was preparing to file a suit against the U.S. government for not allowing scientists the right to study Kennewick Man. Together with the archaeologist Dennis J. Stanford, his colleague at the Smithsonian, Owsley galvanized support from six other well-known specialists who studied ancient remains: Robson Bonnichsen, C. Loring Brace, George Gill, C. Vance Haynes, Jr., Richard L. Jantz, and D. Gentry Steele.

They were experts with impressive academic credentials and clout from Arizona, Michigan, Oregon, Texas, Tennessee, and Wyoming, and they entered the suit as private citizens. In legal terms, the group became known as Bonnichsen—since, alphabetically, the name Robson Bonnichsen came first. Partly because Chatters felt his prior involvement with the skeleton might hurt the case, he did not join the collaboration.

On October 16, 1996, in the U.S. District Court for the District of Oregon in Portland, lawyers for the eight scientists—the plaintiffs—began the case of *Bonnichsen et al v. the United States of America*. Many people following the trial misunderstood what it was about. It did not pit scientists against Native Americans; none of the five tribes was directly involved. Rather, the case was about whether the government had made a mistake in promising the skeleton to the tribes. The government had not correctly followed the law, the scientists argued, and so they should have full access to the ancient skeleton for purposes of study.

The case was complicated, and lawyers on both sides could see that it would be a long and laborious process and that no one could foretell what the final outcome would be.

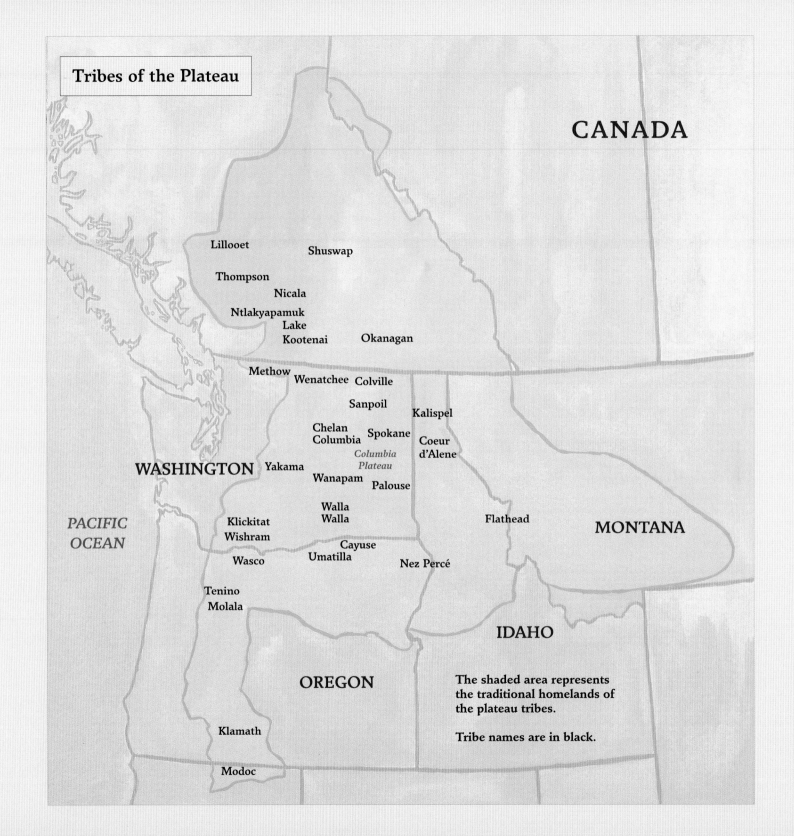

# Tribes of the Plateau

CANADA

Lillooet     Shuswap

Thompson

Nicala

Ntlakyapamuk
Lake
Kootenai     Okanagan

Methow
Wenatchee   Colville

Sanpoil

Kalispel

Chelan   Spokane
Columbia         Coeur
d'Alene

*Columbia
Plateau*

WASHINGTON   Yakama

Wanapam   Palouse

Walla
Walla

Flathead

MONTANA

PACIFIC
OCEAN

Klickitat
Wishram

Cayuse

Wasco    Umatilla

Nez Percé

Tenino
Molala

IDAHO

OREGON

The shaded area represents
the traditional homelands of
the plateau tribes.

Tribe names are in black.

Klamath

Modoc

14

**Northwest United States and Canada**

**South-Central Washington**

**Kennewick and the Tri-Cities Area**

## Native Americans of the Plateau

The tribes of the Columbia Plateau live in the western parts of Canada, eastern Washington and Oregon, north-central Idaho, and western Montana. For thousands of years their ancestors survived as hunter-gathers in this semiarid region of grassland and sagebrush nourished by the Columbia River and bordered by the Cascade Range and the Rocky Mountains.

In 1805, the Lewis and Clark expedition arrived on the Columbia Plateau, ushering in an era of contact with European settlers. In the Kennewick area, Walla Walla chief Yelleppit (or Yelépt) traded a white horse to Clark for his sword. Soon after, fur traders and missionaries settled on the plateau. With them came diseases like smallpox, cholera, and measles, for which the native people did not have immunity. Epidemics nearly wiped out entire villages.

Both British and American fur trappers and traders established trading forts in the region. In 1846, the United States and Great Britain made an agreement, and the lands of the Oregon Territory (now Washington, Oregon, Idaho, and western Montana) became the property of the United States. Four years later, in 1850, Congress passed the Donation Land Claim Act, which permitted any U.S. citizen to claim up to 320 acres in the Oregon Territory. This included land where Native Americans already lived. The Oregon Trail, the route many settlers took to come west, cut directly across tribal homegrounds.

In 1853, Congress further divided the Oregon Territory, creating the Washington Territory from it, and Isaac Stevens became the region's first governor. To create room for more white settlers, Stevens set out to make treaties with the plateau tribes and move them onto reservations. The government officials negotiating the treaties threatened war if their proposals were not accepted by the Native Americans. The plateau tribes lost 64 million acres of land when they signed the treaties. Tribal leaders refused, however, to give up the right to hunt and fish in their accustomed locations (a guarantee that continues to be of legal and political significance today). Not all the tribal groups signed treaties, but all were moved to reservations.

The tribal territories are presented here as they were mapped in the early 1800s. Today, most of the modern-day plateau tribes continue to occupy portions of their traditional homelands.

# A Nine-Year Court Battle

The scientists' argument took shape. They insisted that giving Kennewick Man to the tribes was not legal under NAGPRA. They further argued that the Corps had violated federal procedures regarding NAGPRA. The skeleton was so old that he could not possibly be identified by law as an ancestor of any modern-day group. Kennewick Man's link to any twentieth-century tribe or tribes, Owsley and his colleagues asserted, could not be scientifically established; physical characteristics showed that the skeleton was not biologically related to any Native Americans living today. The scientists' suit concluded that Kennewick Man was not Native American under the law—and that even if he were, there was nothing in NAGPRA that prevented his remains from being studied.

Lawyers for the Corps—the defense—counterargued that, as defined by NAGPRA, any skeleton older than Christopher Columbus's arrival in the Americas in 1492 is automatically classified as Native American. Since the Ancient One had lived far earlier than any accepted legal record of Europeans in North America—Columbus or the Vikings or anyone else—he had to be recognized by law as Native American. Under this interpretation, it didn't matter how recently the Umatilla or other tribes had moved into the Columbia River Basin, nor did it matter whether the skeleton was culturally or biologically related to them.

Nor, the defense continued, did NAGPRA require scientific proof. The five tribes, through their oral histories and the geography, were clearly indigenous. So giving custody of the skeleton to the five tribes fell entirely within the law. If the tribes did not wish to have the skeleton studied, it was their legal right to repatriate it—to bring it within their own peoples' laws and customs—immediately.

During the first year of the trial, in a surprising twist of events, the Asatru Folk Assembly, a neo-pagan religious group, filed suit against the government for custody of the Ancient One. Aiming to help the scientists win the right to study the skeleton, the Asatru claimed that Kennewick Man was an ancestor related not to Native American groups but to them, a group with Germanic ties. They had reviewed Chatters's description of the skull's shape and interpreted the information to mean that Kennewick Man was of European descent. The ancient man, therefore, was one of their own forebears who had come to the Pacific Northwest more than 9,000 years ago. The court dismissed the Asatru's suit because of a lack of evidence.

Newspapers would eventually carry photos of the Asatru's leader Stephen McNallen, resembling a Viking with his long beard and cloak, pouring libations from a spiraling ox horn. Umatilla religious leader Armand Minthorn, who wore his long hair in braids, would inadvertently (and much to his chagrin) become a media personality, too. No image caught the public's eye, however, as much as the Ancient One's did.

As the trial continued, a bust of Kennewick Man's face

# A Face for Kennewick Man

An artist created these illustrations of Kennewick Man's face based on a cast that was made of his skull. Changing his hairstyle and eyebrows alters our concept of what he may have looked like. The turn of the lip, the angle of an eyelid, or the presence or absence of facial hair changes our impression of him, and can affect what we see.

These interpretations are not meant to be entirely realistic. As well as demonstrating possibilities for facial construction, this illustration depicts how the Ancient One was stereotyped in the media.

made by Chatters and artist Tom McClelland, based on a cast of the skull, appeared in *The New Yorker*. People looked at it, and each saw something different. Some said the face resembled Patrick Stewart of *Star Trek* fame. Others said the bust favored the legendary Chief Joseph of the Nez Percé.

Artists' renditions of the ancient man's face appeared on the cover of *Time* and in the pages of *Newsweek* and *National Geographic*. Each illustrator gave him a contrasting appearance; on *Time*'s cover, the Ancient One looked Asian. Kennewick Man's age and ambiguous ancestry, along with the question of repatriation and reburial, continued to inspire passionate debates. He became the subject of a half dozen books, several documentary films, TV programs such as *Nova* and *60 Minutes*, and many websites.

Kennewick Man continued to capture headlines as other events, both inside and outside the courtroom, transpired. Newspapers reported that on several occasions in 1997, the Corps permitted the five tribes, as well as members of the Asatru Folk Assembly, to perform "ceremonies" over the bones. What exactly happened remains disputed; what is known for sure is that members of these groups were present in the room at Battelle when the Corps performed curatorial work on the Ancient One.

Another incident caused even more controversy. An inventory made by the Corps showed that parts of Kennewick Man's skeleton had disappeared. Corps archaeologists compared the bones to the photographs Jim Chatters had made more than two years earlier and determined that portions of one of the large femur bones were missing. According to one story, a janitor in the Benton County sheriff's office had stolen the bones after authorities removed them from Jim Chatters's lab. Other rumors cited Chatters himself or the Umatilla as suspects. In the end, no one was charged with theft and the bones were later mysteriously found when the sheriff's department moved its evidence locker to a new location.

The Battelle facility was not secure enough to house Kennewick Man, the Corps decided. The Corps chose the Burke Museum of Natural History and Culture, on the campus of the University of Washington in Seattle, as a safe place for the bones. There they would be kept in a temperature- and humidity-monitored room in one of the storage areas of the museum's lower levels. Each bone would be put in protective casing and placed within boxes with other bones according to anatomical grouping. All the bones from the left hand fit into one box, while all of the bones from the right hand fit into another box. The bones belonging to each hand were grouped together, likewise the pieces of the pelvis, the bones of the left rib cage, the bones of the right rib cage, and so on. The Corps agreed to pay for the storage and care of the bones. Kennewick Man arrived in Seattle on October 29, 1998.

Four months later, as the trial continued, the Corps revisited the decision it had made about Kennewick Man, this time after consulting with scientific experts. Hired by a different branch of the federal government, the U.S. Department of the Interior, were five physical anthropologists from universities in Arkansas, Arizona, New Mexico, and Washington State. They came to the Burke to learn what they could about the skeleton's cultural affiliation. These scientists were a different group from the plaintiffs in the lawsuit.

The scientists measured and remeasured Kennewick Man's skull and other skeletal pieces. To the great distress of the tribes, the scientists took new samples of bone for radiocarbon testing and DNA analysis. A new radiocarbon test reconfirmed the skeleton to be 9,300–9,500 years old.

## Facial Reconstruction

Forensic art blends art with known facts. Forensic drawings or sculptures are usually made for purposes of identification. One form of forensic art, in which a sculpture of a face is re-created using the measurements of the skull, is called "facial reconstruction." Historians and archaeologists like to have facial reconstructions made to find out what ancient people might have looked like in life. Facial reconstructions are becoming increasingly popular in museum work, as mummies and skeletons are taken off display because of human-rights issues. In cases where the remains have been reburied, the bust provides a way to represent and remember the individual.

How accurate are facial reconstructions? A physical anthropologist or forensic artist with an excellent knowledge of anatomy can sometimes create an image accurate enough for a real person to be identified from it. However, the process of creating an image from a skull is far from exact. There are many variables. Without visual aids like a photograph of the living person or a genetic test that indicates ancestry, an artist must imagine such details as the size and shape of the lips, nose, and ears. Errors can easily be made.

To the trained eye of a physical anthropologist, the shape of a skull can indicate general possibilities. But it cannot absolutely confirm a person's ancestry or race. (*See* "Why Study Skeletons?" and "What Is Race?" sidebars.)

**What can be determined from a skull:**
> Proportional arrangements of facial features
> Approximate age
> Sex
> Teeth, individual characteristics and conditions
> Injuries, malnutrition, and other possible illnesses
> Approximate weight
> Possible indicators of ancestry

**What cannot be determined from a skull:**
> Skin color and freckles or other markings
> Wrinkles or other lines on skin
> Hair color, type, and style
> Facial hair (such as mustache or beard)
> Eyebrows and eyelid structure
> Eye color
> Shape and length of nose
> Shape of ears
> Shape of lips and mouth

As before, the DNA tests proved inconclusive, as none of the samples contained enough genetic material to produce results.

After a week of intense studying, the five scientists concluded that Kennewick Man could not be linked with any certainty to any population currently alive in the world. Though he was almost certainly a Paleoindian, indigenous to the Americas, proving a direct line of descent would be impossible.

More than another year went by before the Department of the Interior released its own conclusions. On September 24, 2000, Interior Secretary Bruce Babbitt announced his support for the Corps' original decision. Cultural and geographic connections tied the remains of Kennewick Man to the five tribes, he said, and he declared that the skeleton should be turned over to the tribes for reburial.

This announcement appeared to be a triumph for the tribes. However, in Portland, the trial was still going on. At the end of 2001, the two sides delivered some 22,000 pages of documents to Judge John Jelderks. He promised to read every page.

On August 30, 2002, more than six years after the discovery of the skeleton, Judge Jelderks announced his decision. He'd heard the testimony of two dozen government lawyers, close to fifty members of the scientific community, engineers, the tribes, and a range of other witnesses. He'd sifted through a staggering amount of evidence. (Legal experts estimated that the United States had spent about three million dollars defending the case.)

Judge Jelderks posted his judgment on the federal court's Electronic Case Filing system, which sent word by e-mail to the lawyers for the two sides. The seventy-six-page document said, in effect: Kennewick Man is not Native American under the specific definition of the law; the plaintiffs' request to study the skeleton is granted. In his interpretation, the remains did not qualify as Native American under NAGPRA because no link to an existing Native American group could be established.

The scientists had won.

In the following months, the scientists and their teams submitted detailed research requests to the Corps. At the same time, the tribes appealed the court's decision. After a three-judge panel on the U.S. Court of Appeals for the Ninth Circuit upheld the district court's opinion, the U.S. government and the tribes decided not to take further legal action. An appeal to the U.S. Supreme Court on their own would have cost the tribes a lot of money—and there was no guarantee that the Court would even hear the case.

The Corps approved the scientists' study plans. Working in small groups, under supervision, each scientist would be able to conduct studies of the bones for designated periods of a day or two. For the plaintiffs, who'd waited for so long to view the bones and research the mysteries and secrets of prehistoric humans, the outcome was a great relief.

# Kennewick Man and DNA Testing

A person can be identified from a drop of blood or a single hair, distinguishing him or her from all the people who have ever lived. Starting in the 1980s, such a feat became possible through DNA testing, which involves the study of deoxyribonucleic acid found in the cells of all living things.

DNA evidence can help investigators solve crimes. Scientists who study Kennewick Man, however, have a different purpose for wanting to analyze his DNA. They hope that DNA testing will give clues to his ancestry.

Genetics is the study of how living things inherit features, or traits—such as hair color or eye color—from their ancestors. Genetic information is carried by the DNA molecule. This long molecule duplicates in the cells of the individual and is passed down from parents to children. Individual segments of DNA are called "genes."

Most of the DNA in a human being's genes is the same from one person to another, but in a few places there are differences in the sequence or the length of the DNA. Scientists can measure these differences and use them as markers, or indicators, to establish how closely people are related.

When people migrated from one part of the world to another in ancient times, they carried in their cells genetic patterns of their ancestors. Today, scientists can see differences in the DNA of populations living in different parts of the world.

DNA sequences gradually alter over time because of random, sudden changes called "mutations." As groups of people become separated over hundreds and thousands of years, the mutations accumulate. When a population is descended from a small group of ancestors, some DNA markers can become more common or less common owing to chance alone. This is called "genetic drift."

By looking at the frequencies of many different DNA markers, scientists can estimate from what part of the world a person's ancestors probably came. If DNA could be obtained from Kennewick Man, scientists would compare it with a vast database of samples from millions of people, both living and deceased. DNA testing of Kennewick Man could show how closely related he is—or isn't—to other ancient populations and their descendants.

But so far, bone samples taken from Kennewick Man and sent for DNA testing have not shown any results. Testing on ancient bone samples is very difficult. Though DNA can be found in bones and teeth, it is found far more easily in blood, hair, urine, skin tissue, or organs such as the brain. And the older the bone, the more likely the DNA inside it has become damaged. All cell matter degrades, or breaks down, over time, which is probably why DNA could not be found in several of Kennewick Man's bone samples.

Another challenge for scientists is that they often find that bone samples are contaminated. The DNA of living people who handle bones or the DNA of animals that came in contact with bones when they were in the soil can sabotage test results.

For these reasons, it's not known whether doing more DNA testing on Kennewick Man would yield results. Still, scientists continue to develop new and more sophisticated DNA tests. In the future, if scientists are given permission to take more samples from Kennewick Man for testing, they will once again try their skills on the Ancient One's bony matter and hope for conclusive results.

# The Scientists Study
# the Skeleton

On a hot, sunny day in Seattle, in July 2005, children climbed on the graceful Native American sculpture of an orca whale outside the University of Washington's Burke Museum. Visitors admired the intricately carved, earth-red and sky-blue totem poles. Inside there was a long showcase of gems and minerals, mounted birds, and eggs. The visitors gazed at the ceiling, fascinated by an enormous fossil fish.

It was a day much like any other at the Burke, except that among the visitors were some of the plaintiffs in *Bonnichsen*

*et al v. the United States of America*. The scientists arrived in the basement through a side entrance, an area not open to the public, and vanished behind locked doors. There they would confront a treasure. After nine long years, the scientists had finally come to study Kennewick Man.

Jim Chatters was now working with the scientists who had prevailed in the court case. A team of about twenty-five

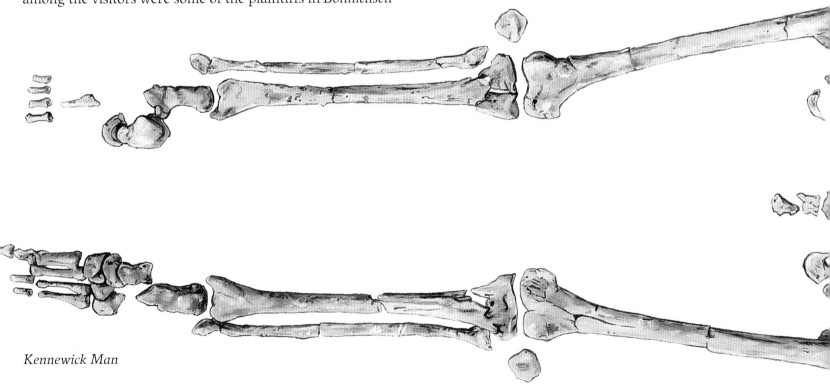

*Kennewick Man*

experts planned to visit the museum, some in July 2005 and others in February 2006. Following the terms decreed by the Corps, curators from both the Corps and the Burke Museum were on hand to supervise the scientists. Several scientists would visit the skeleton on more than one day, depending on their study plans. Most had been allotted only a few hours.

As Chatters, the Smithsonian anthropologist Doug Owsley, and others looked on, the museum curators carefully opened the boxes containing Kennewick Man's bones. The boxes were then arranged on tables according to their anatomical position in the body. Then the scientists took turns studying the bones and removed them from their foam cases as needed.

Some bones still carried dirt from the riverbed, which no one had washed off. Whenever a piece of dirt fell, or a tiny flake of the bone fell off, a curator labeled it and saved it in a plastic bag for potential future study and to ensure

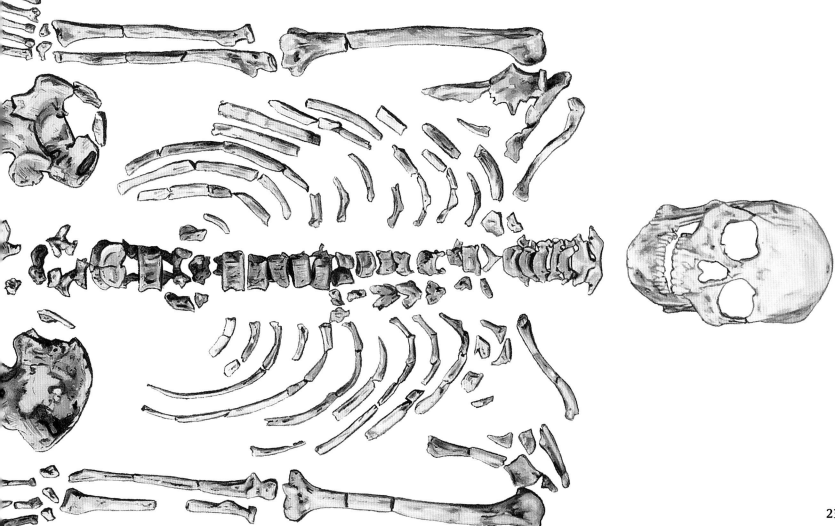

that the bone fragments were kept together out of respect for the dead. As directed by the Corps, the curators and scientists handling the bones wore cotton or synthetic gloves, and all refrained from wearing jewelry, since ancient bones crack and flake easily and need to be handled with great care.

Robson Bonnichsen, whose name headed the legal documents, did not join the other plaintiffs at the Burke Museum that July. He had died the previous December. A chronic illness prevented another of the plaintiffs from studying the skeleton. The lawsuit had been so time-consuming that by its conclusion some of the other scientists had reached retirement age. Their victory had been bittersweet.

Even so, the scientists who now viewed the skeleton for the first time were elated to be in its presence. In the words of physical anthropologist Richard L. Jantz, "Nothing was like seeing the real thing." The scientists marveled at the Ancient One's incredible robustness. As the experts who'd previously seen Kennewick Man had already noted, his bone mass showed he'd been very muscular and strong. His right arm and shoulder had been built up, probably from throwing spears.

Jantz and others measured Kennewick Man's bones with new high-tech tools, such as a three-dimensional digitizer, a handheld laser scanner. The scanners could almost instantly—at approximately two seconds per shot—measure angles, area depth, shapes, and thickness with the highest level of accuracy. The data would be used to create three-dimensional models on computer screens and in plastic.

Doug Owsley confirmed earlier findings that the ancient man had been about five feet nine or ten inches

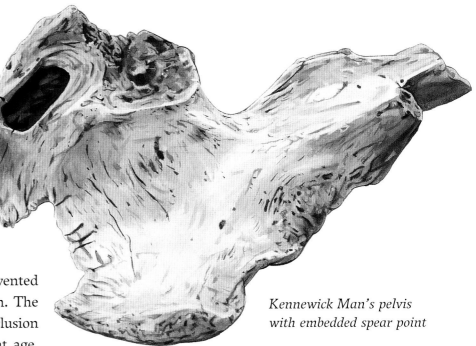

*Kennewick Man's pelvis with embedded spear point*

tall and right-handed. He had had arthritis in both knees as well as in his right elbow and in some vertebrae, possibly as a result of frequent squatting and kneeling. The position of the stone point in his hip, Owsley observed, showed that the Ancient One had been hit from the front by an assailant throwing a spear from many yards away. The hip bone had grown back around the spear point: The injury had not been fatal. Likewise, the man's head injury hadn't killed him.

Previously, scientists had estimated that the Ancient One was forty to fifty-five years old when he died. Owsley believed that he could have been as young as thirty-eight. Owsley also looked at the shape of the bones and found calcium deposits. He concluded that Kennewick Man had intentionally been buried on his back with his arms at his sides and his palms facing down. Over the centuries, until recent floods dislodged him, his skeleton was aligned with the riverbank. The river was on his left side, and his head was positioned upstream. But the cause of Kennewick

Man's death remained a mystery—there are some stories that bones alone cannot reveal.

The Ancient One wasn't missing any teeth and didn't have a single cavity. These facts were already well-known but still captured the attention of the scientists who had rarely viewed such a complete ancient skull. The way Kennewick Man's teeth were worn led Chatters to the conclusion that he'd probably gripped slabs of meat or sinew in his teeth. Chatters pictured Kennewick Man eating in just this practical way, with one hand holding the meat while the other cut the food with a sharp stone knife.

Did the ancient man's skull proportions come mostly from his lifestyle? Or were the proportions strictly due to heredity? Later, in the quiet of his home office, Chatters pondered the data. Perhaps the repeated pulling motions while eating gave Kennewick Man his overbite and even elongated his face.

What kinds of fibrous or sandy foods had ground down Kennewick Man's teeth? Thomas Stafford, an anthropologist and laboratory scientist, cut tiny samples from selected bones, as his approved study plan allowed him to. Later, in his Colorado lab, Stafford would preform isotope testing, or study the chemical composition of these bone fragments, to see whether he could shed any light on this question. So far the data has not yielded results, though someday it may be possible for Stanford to determine whether the Ancient One ate mostly fish or meat.

Knowing more about Kennewick Man's food sources would give the scientists clues about other aspects of his life, such as where Kennewick Man lived and traveled. Maybe the data would even reveal whether he had begun his life somewhere other than the Pacific Northwest.

As the scientists studied the skull fractures, examined the spear point in Kennewick Man's hip, and made notes, cameras flashed. Chip Clark, a well-known photographer, had come from the Smithsonian with Owsley. Alan Schneider of Portland, the principal lawyer involved in handling the scientists' legal case, also watched.

When a space became available at a table, another scientist moved into it and studied the skull. Jantz took the measurements that he'd add to a giant computer database to compare Kennewick Man's skull with skulls from all over the world and different time periods. The data would be examined to try to identify who the first inhabitants of the Americas were, when they had arrived on this continent, and from where.

Later, after comparing measurements of many skulls, Jantz and Owsley concluded that the first humans probably arrived in North America by a sea route along the west coast from Asia, rather than by way of an overland route across the Bering Land Bridge. Individual crania, or skulls, are highly variable—each person has his or her own

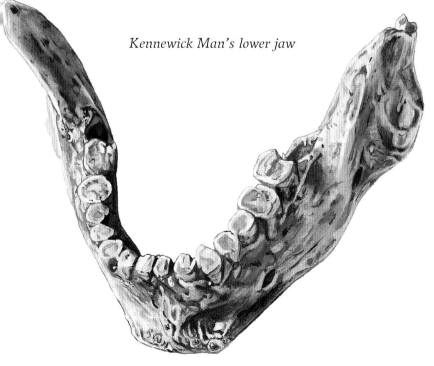

*Kennewick Man's lower jaw*

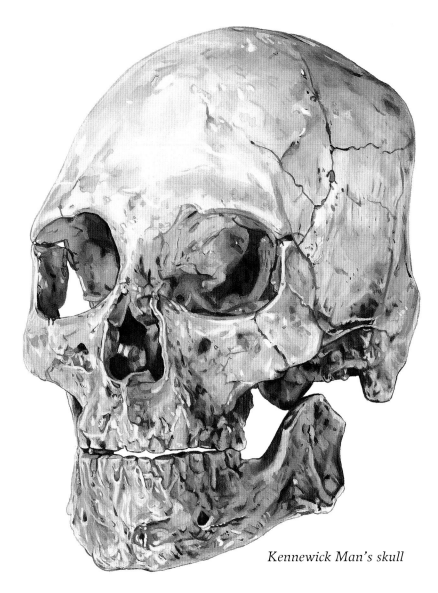

*Kennewick Man's skull*

muscle marks and evidence of injuries that Kennewick Man had endured during his lifetime. Later he would create a computer animation, like the analysis of a champion athlete, showing Kennewick Man's throwing motion.

Chatters studied the enlarged right shoulder bone. In the months to come, after sharing his observations with medical specialists, he'd conclude that the ancient man had suffered from shoulder pain. Like some baseball players, Kennewick Man had a bony outgrowth on the socket of his shoulder blade, caused by repeated pressure from the upper arm—a condition known as "thrower's exostosis" or "thrower's shoulder." If he'd lived in modern times, a doctor might have advised surgery. The ancient hunter did not rest when he was injured but kept on throwing. That's why his shoulder and his ribs failed to heal perfectly. His likely targets were deer, elk, and bison; his throwing motion suggested a lifetime of big-game hunting with a projectile and spear.

Chatters's studies of Kennewick Man's leg bones showed that his pelvic injury had not interfered with his gait. Though the point remained lodged in his hip, the ancient man didn't limp. If his pelvic injury had occurred during his childhood, when his bones were still growing, rather than in his adult years, its effects would have been greater.

So far, no DNA had been found when fragments of Kennewick Man's bones were analyzed by several different labs. There was the possibility of a successful DNA test, some scientists felt, if they could scoop out the interior of a tooth or large bone, but the Corps did not permit such samples to be taken during this current phase of studies. Part of the team's research now focused on assessing which bones, or parts of bones, might yield DNA if sampled in the future. Ideally, the scientists hoped to get results by using only a very small portion of bone material.

uniquely shaped head. But to Jantz and Owsley, the skulls from the ancient skeletons found in western North America, especially in their large cranial capacity, or "vault" size, tended to most resemble those of the Asian Pacific Rim.

It was Chatters's goal to learn more about the ancient man's lifestyle by studying his muscle development as seen by the shapes of his bones. Chatters focused on re-recording data, cross-checking earlier notes, and photographing

In the future, increasingly sensitive tests being developed by Stafford and others would make such a feat possible.

Throughout the day, the members of the study group took turns with the bones at the three tables. The scientists concentrated so intently on their work that all too soon the day was gone. Afterward, the curators carefully packed Kennewick Man away and took him to his private, secret room in the building.

The data gathered at the Burke Museum supplied the scientists with ideas to think about in the months and years to come. Archaeology, like all disciplines of learning, is an unfolding process. For this scientific team, the profound rewards of their profession come from pinning down answers to questions—questions such as who the Ancient One's ancestors might have been. But simply coming closer to answering such questions is also satisfying. Discovering a new piece to a difficult puzzle is often the high point of a scientific career.

# Theories and Findings

As of the publication of this book, the plaintiff scientists who studied Kennewick Man have not yet reported their findings to the Corps, or in scholarly, peer-reviewed research papers. However, several of the scientists have presented some of their findings in other articles and in public symposiums. The scientists continue to suggest that although Kennewick Man does not belong to any modern ethnic group, his bone measurements resemble those of Polynesians and the Ainu, a generally light-skinned (though not Caucasian) people. The Ainu are credited as being the first settlers of Japan. The Polynesians, Ainu, and Kennewick Man's people may have evolved from a common ancestor thousands of years ago.

Charles Loring Brace, a physical anthropologist, believes that Kennewick Man's folk descended from the Jomon, an ancient people who lived in Siberia, Manchuria, and the northern portions of Japan. The seafaring Jomon traveled long distances in canoes made of planks. They ate sea mammals. The Jomon's descendants, Brace thinks, eventually spread across the woodlands of what is now Canada and the northwestern United States.

There is still no information available about the Ancient One's genetic makeup. But recent genetic studies of other skeletal remains and of human coprolites (feces) confirm the theory that the first humans in North America came from Asia. The studies show that modern-day Native Americans and the ancient Paleoindians (at least according to the remains in which DNA could be found) belong to the same genetic grouping. This grouping includes people of Asian origin, and it differs entirely from the genetic branch that includes individuals of European background. In other words, the Ancient One is very likely related to modern-day Native Americans (although he isn't necessarily "Native American" by legal definition according to NAGPRA, as Judge Jelderks and others have asserted).

But why the skeleton of Kennewick Man looks different from modern-day Native Americans continues to be a subject of debate among scientists. Other ancient skeletons found in North America also look different from Native Americans of the past few hundred years. These include the Spirit Cave Mummy, the 9,400-year-old remains of a man found in Nevada, and Buhl Woman, a 12,400-year-old skeleton of a young woman found in Idaho. Like the Ancient One, they each have a high, narrow cranium, relatively narrow cheekbones, and a "forward-positioned" face. In contrast, Native American and Asian skulls have shorter, rounder craniums and broader, flatter faces.

Jantz and Owsley see these physical differences as evidence of "ethnic replacement"—the process whereby one group of people replaces another. They suggest that various bands of people migrated from Asia to North America at different times. The smallest bands either died out or gradually disappeared through intermarriage with a far larger band.

Another anthropologist, Joseph Powell, suggests an alternative explanation. He sees one initial migration

## The Spirit Cave Mummy

In 1940, while conducting an excavation in the Grimes Point foothills near Fallon, Nevada, archaeologists Sydney and Georgia Wheeler discovered a variety of human remains in a cave. They found cremated remains in bags woven from twisted reeds and grasses. Beside the bags, they found a trench where the cremations had likely taken place.

While digging just below surface soil in another part of the cave, the Wheelers came upon two large, very skillfully woven reed body sacks, one placed on top of the other. The top one contained just a few bones, but the bottom sack held a body that was part skeleton, part mummy, with some remaining skin and hair. The ancient man's remains had been naturally mummified by the hot, dry climate of the desert. He was dressed in a cloak made of strands of twined rabbit fur, and he wore skin moccasins.

The Wheelers took the Spirit Cave Mummy, as the remains have come to be known, to the Nevada State Museum in 1940. They estimated him to be a thousand to two thousand years old. It was not until 1996, when museum staff performed radiocarbon dating on the Spirit Cave Mummy, that they found, to their great surprise, that he was 9,400 years old—among the oldest remains ever found in North America and by far the best preserved.

That year, the Bureau of Land Management (BLM), a government agency that retains custody of the Spirit Cave Mummy, allowed Doug Owsley, Richard Jantz, and other physical anthropologists to study the skeleton. Because of objections from local Native Americans, the BLM would not allow DNA testing. By examining the remains, the physical anthropologists determined that the mummy was of a man who had lived to be between thirty-five to fifty-five years old. He'd been born with an abnormal spine, a genetic defect of having an extra vertebra, which probably caused him lower-back pain.

His skull showed that he had a partially healed wound on his right temple, a blow that occurred a month or more before his death. He had all his teeth, though they were worn down, several down to the pulp and holed by abscesses. These infections, Owsley concluded, likely killed the man. Studies of the food remains in the man's inner organs showed that his last meal included numerous small fish, probably swallowed whole. Pollen in the stools indicated he could also have eaten seeds or the fibers of marsh plants.

In 1997, on behalf of all Northern Paiute tribal governments, the Fallon Paiute Shoshone Tribe claimed the Spirit Cave Mummy under NAGPRA. In 1998, the BLM determined that the remains were Native American but were too old to be affiliated with any tribal group living today. The Fallon Paiute Shoshone Tribe disagreed and sued the BLM in federal district court.

The case is still ongoing. Owsley and others—some of the same plaintiffs involved in studying Kennewick Man—want to conduct DNA testing on the Spirit Cave Mummy.

This situation is different from that of Kennewick Man in several respects. Both parties agree that the remains are Native American, extensive study was allowed prior to the court case, and the remains were found prior to the passing of NAGPRA (so a different section of NAGPRA applies).

from Asia, a "parent group," which fanned out into small bands. As the bands spread across America, they lost contact with one another. The small, isolated groups, Powell says, encountered unique climates and other specific conditions and, after a while, evolved separately.

Chatters concludes that both of these viewpoints may be correct. His theory is that all the native peoples in North and South America came from the same parent population in Asia. Isolated from the rest of humanity, they lived for at least 5,000 years on an icy strip of land called Beringia, which once connected Asia with North America. Eventually, one or more bands left Beringia. Another group remained in that Arctic-like environment and evolved broad, flat faces in response to the harsh weather conditions. This band, he suggests, later emigrated to North America and replaced the earlier band or bands.

## More Mysteries

The Ancient One lived during a time of sweeping environmental and technological change. Between 9,500 and 9,000 years ago, the seasonal climate that Kennewick Man knew, with hot summers and very cold winters, became drier and more temperate. As massive ice sheets over Canada and Alaska melted, sea levels rose along the coast. On the Columbia Plateau, the large grassland areas began to turn into a more desertlike environment. At the same time, the mountains became more forested. The Douglas fir, which dotted the Cascade Range, spread to the lower slopes. The populations of deer, elk, and giant bison shrank in size as their grazing land receded.

Meanwhile, rivers like the Columbia flowed at lower levels. Salmon runs increased as the new forests began to shadow and cool the upper parts of the rivers. As fish and shellfish became more abundant, a new and different way of life along the river would become dominant. A lifestyle based on big game hunting gave way to a lifestyle that relied more on smaller game hunting, fishing, and collecting plants.

Artifacts found on and around the Columbia Plateau in dozens of archaeological digs show two distinct traditions, one from before 9,000 years ago, the other after that time. The groups differed in their use of the land, where and how they settled, how they hunted, the tools they used, and what they ate. Their sandal styles and possibly their clothing styles varied as well.

The Ancient One lived when both traditions faced each other across the Cascade Mountain range. Archaeologists call the earlier tradition the Western Stemmed Tradition (also known locally on the Columbia Plateau as Windust). These hunter-gatherers moved hundreds of miles in seasonal journeys, and returned to familiar camps year after year. In summer, they trekked to high mountain camps where they hunted elk, deer, a giant and now extinct form of bison, and marmots, a form of groundhog. In the fall and winter, they followed the big game to lowland areas, wetlands and grasslands near lakes and rivers. There they also hunted birds and rabbits.

The Western Stemmed folk fashioned different tools for hunting various kinds of game. The people's favored tool—the tool that is most characteristic of these people and gives them their name—is a long, broad spear point that tapers, or "stems," to a flat or rounded base. (*See* "Kennewick Man's Tool Kit" sidebar for examples.) They made their spear points by a method archaeologists call

# Clovis Mystery

One of the most interesting—and controversial—areas of North American archaeology involves the Clovis people, the Ice Age hunter-gatherers who once trekked across North America. These Paleoindians made large, flat, beautifully crafted spear points, which they used for killing mammoths as well as smaller animals. Both the hunters and the points they made are now called Clovis, after a site in New Mexico where the first spear points of this type were found.

Clovis sites dot the continent and date from around 11,200 to 10,900 years ago. That's about two thousand years before Kennewick Man was born. Mysteriously, after inhabiting North America for about three hundred years, the Clovis people appear to have vanished. Or at least their need to make distinctive Clovis points disappeared.

The ancient hunters who came after the Clovis people fashioned smaller and often more crudely made spear points. (*See* "Kennewick Man's Tool Kit" sidebar.) No one knows why the newer technology differed—and seemed to have regressed—from what preceded it.

The Clovis culture disappeared at the same time giant mammals like the mammoth and the saber-toothed tiger became extinct—another mystery. The Ice Age giants may have died out because the Clovis people overhunted them. Or more likely the warming climate made survival impossible for these cold-loving animals.

For many years, beginning in the 1930s, archaeologists believed the Clovis people to be America's most ancient ancestors. According to one theory, the Clovis people entered North America from Asia on the Bering Land Bridge around 13,500 years ago. Before this time, scientists said, around 14,000 to 18,000 years ago, migrations could not have taken place over land because ice sheets covered the area of present-day Canada.

But sites such as the Paisley Caves in Oregon and Monte Verde in Chile indicate that ancient man arrived in the Americas at least 14,000 and possibly as long ago as 20,000 years. These new dates puzzle archaeologists. They continue to come up with new theories about how, where, and when humans set foot in North America.

The earliest Paleoindians left few traces of their existence. So each time scientists uncover evidence—such as a firepit, an ancient footprint, butchered mastodon bones, or fossilized human feces—there's much excitement among the anthropological community. Every new discovery has the potential of offering new clues about the evolution and migrations of ancient populations.

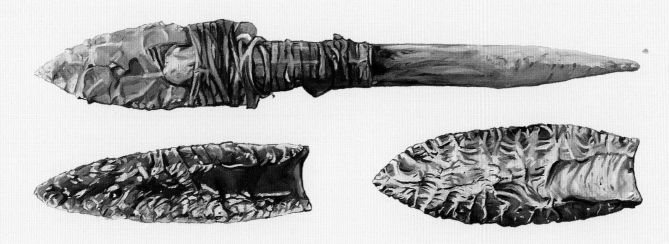

*Clovis Points*

"flint knapping"—reducing stones to a desired shape by striking them and breaking off pieces, or flakes. First they used a large oval stone, or hammerstone, to break off larger flakes from the original stone mass. Then with a pointy tool, such as an antler, they further shaped and refined the stone into a spear point.

The wear patterns on the spear points show that some were used for butchering and cutting meat as well as for hunting. Hunters frequently resharpened the points. Archaeologists know this because of scar patterns on the points. Scars overlap those that were originally made when the points were created. By studying patterns of flake scars a specialist can often reconstruct the entire use-life of the artifact.

The Western Stemmed hunters fitted their points into short wooden or bone holders called foreshafts. They probably attached, or hafted, the points to the foreshafts with string made of animal guts called sinew. The foreshaft fitted into a socket in the end of the spear shaft, which was made of wood. This spear shaft fitted into a throwing stick called an atlatl. The atlatl helped the hunter to throw his spear with great force and speed.

The Western Stemmed folk made other tools as well: scrapers for removing the meat from hides, drills for puncturing holes in skins. They sewed their clothing of furs and skins with bone needles a little larger than modern sewing needles. Small stones, chipped into crescent shapes, have also been discovered in the Western Stemmed hunters' upland camps. However, the purpose of these mysterious tools or weapons remains unknown

Another unusual feature of the Western Stemmed tool kit is a round, egg-sized stone. The hunters sometimes grooved the stones so that twine could easily be tied around them. The stones were then tied into groups of two or three. The result was a weapon, called a bola, that could be thrown. These weapons, which spun when thrown through the air, were probably hurled at long-legged birds. Archaeologists have found bola stones only near wetlands and along rivers. Oddly, little evidence of fishing has been found in any of the Western Stemmed camps. It seems that fish did not make up a major part of the diet.

No earth ovens have been found at Western Stemmed sites, either. Nor have archaeologists found "boiling stones"—stones used for heating water. These people apparently roasted—rather than boiled—their meat and other foods. They may have used cooking only as a way to thaw frozen provisions. The wear patterns on Kennewick Man's teeth indicate that he and his people ate tough, dried, or partially cooked meat that they held with their hands and teeth to cut off bites, perhaps with their knives or spear points.

At Western Stemmed sites in the Great Basin area, south of the Columbia Plateau, archaeologists have found basket fragments and woven sandals. These 9,200-year-old sandals have an enclosed toe and an open heel, and were held on the foot by cords that were wrapped around the ankle. Perhaps the Ancient One wore sandals like those. (In contrast, the sandals of later peoples in the same region had heel pockets and a more intricate lacing system in which cords were tightened through a series of loops along the sides of the foot.)

The tradition that replaced the Western Stemmed people on the Columbia Plateau is known as the Old Cordilleran or Pebble Tool Tradition. Unlike the earlier people, the Old Cordilleran camped mostly along rivers. They tended to craft small leaf-shaped spear points with pointed bases (*see* "Kennewick Man's Tool Kit" sidebar) and large

# Migrations

No one knows for sure how long ago ancient humans inhabited North America. Scientists think that it was the quest for food—mammoths, caribou, steppe bison, musk oxen, wild horses, and possibly marine animals—that drew the first hunter-gatherers to this continent.

Most scientists agree that these ancient hunters or Paleoindians came from Asia. They arrived in North America at least 14,000 years ago. Some sites suggest they could have arrived as early as 20,000 to 40,000 years ago, but not all archaeologists agree with those dates.

During the peak of the last great Ice Age, between 23,000 and 19,000 years ago, two immense moving ice sheets called glaciers, almost two miles thick in places, covered much of North America. The glaciers formed over thousands of years as snow fell on polar regions and mountains and did not melt. The snow compacted into sheets of ice; and under enormous weight, they started to spread, eventually covering the North Pole and all of present-day Canada. Very cold temperatures prevented the frozen water trapped in glaciers from melting and running into the oceans. With less water in the oceans, sea levels dropped nearly 400 feet in some areas, exposing the sea bottom along coastlines.

The exposed strip of sea bottom in the Bering Strait that connected Asia with North America became a land bridge of cold, dry grassland. The area is located in present-day Russia, Alaska, and Canada. Scientists call this bridge, and nearby areas of ice-free land, Beringia.

For thousands of years, the bridge, nearly 1,000 miles wide, remained fairly dry for extended periods of time, allowing people and animals to live there as well as travel between the two continents. During cooler periods, however, ice sheets refroze and blocked the passage. At the end of the Ice Age, about 14,000 years ago, the glaciers began to melt. As the sea level rose, the Bering Land Bridge disappeared beneath the waves.

One popular theory says that the Paleoindians walked from Asia across the Bering Land Bridge to west-central Canada about 14,000 years ago (or possibly much earlier). Some archaeologists refer to these small bands of hunter-gatherers as the Clovis people. The Paleoindians stayed on this expanse of cold, dry grassland until the edges of two glaciers covering present-day Canada began to melt, leaving a corridor between them. The hunter-gatherers trekked through the passage to reach the North American mainland about 13,500 years ago. There, they prospered on abundant vegetation and animals. Between 12,800 and 11,900 years ago, they spread across the North American continent and may have become ancestors of other Paleoindian peoples. They left behind distinctive stone tools at many sites.

According to the Pacific Rim theory, Ice Age hunter-gatherers paddled small boats from Asia, past the Bering Land Bridge, down the North American coast to the Pacific Northwest. By hugging the coastline, they avoided glaciers and dined on sea life, shorebirds, and vegetation. Some hunters traveled as far as South America. This theory is supported by evidence—human feces, skeletons, stone tools, and even a settlement, Monte Verde in Chile, that dates back 14,000 years ago.

The third theory, called the Solutrean Connection, is not widely accepted by archaeologists. It is named after a Paleolithic or Stone Age culture in western Europe. A few researchers believe hunters left the area that is now Spain in boats about 19,700 years ago. They paddled north along the Atlantic coastline, then traveled west and navigated ice floes to reach North America. Eventually, these early explorers moved south along the coast. Stone tools, similar to those found in Europe, have been found in sites in eastern North America. But a link between these tools and those found in Europe has not clearly been established.

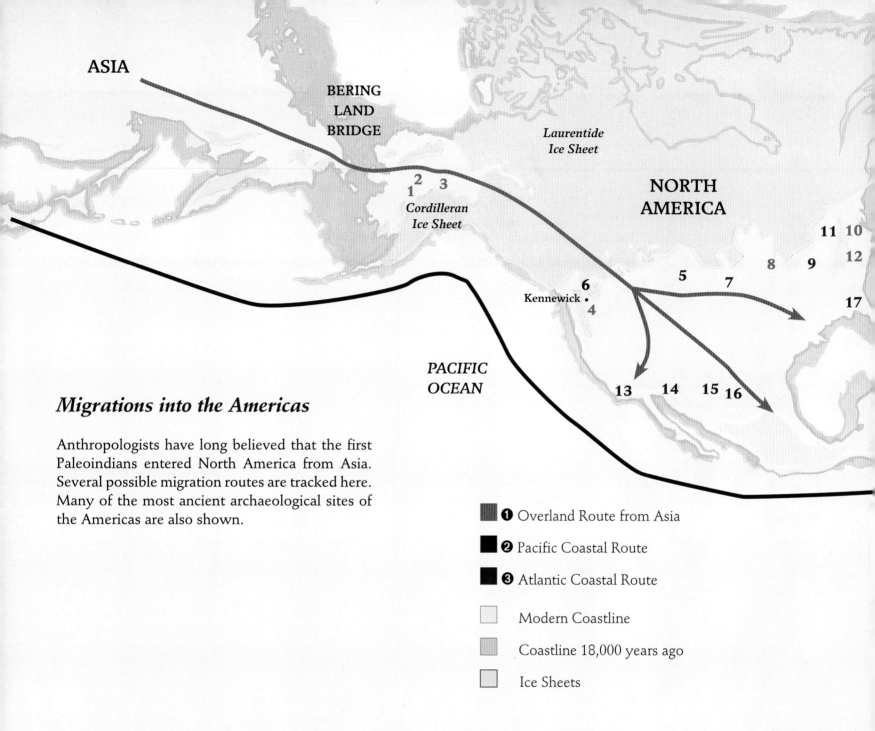

ASIA

BERING
LAND
BRIDGE

Laurentide
Ice Sheet

NORTH
AMERICA

2
1 3
Cordilleran
Ice Sheet

11 10
12
8 9
5 7
17
6
Kennewick •
4

PACIFIC
OCEAN

13 14 15 16

## Migrations into the Americas

Anthropologists have long believed that the first
Paleoindians entered North America from Asia.
Several possible migration routes are tracked here.
Many of the most ancient archaeological sites of
the Americas are also shown.

❶ Overland Route from Asia

❷ Pacific Coastal Route

❸ Atlantic Coastal Route

Modern Coastline

Coastline 18,000 years ago

Ice Sheets

EUROPE →

ATLANTIC
OCEAN

SOUTH
AMERICA

18

19      21

20

22

## Pre-Clovis Sites, or Sites Older than 13,500 Years (13,500–15,500 years old, or possibly as old as 18,000–28,000 years old)

1   Nenana Complex, Alaska
2   Swan Point, Alaska
3   Bluefish Caves, Alaska*
4   Paisley Caves, Oregon
8   Schaefer Mammoth and Hebior Mammoth sites, Wisconsin
10  Meadowcroft Rockshelter, Pennsylvania*
12  Cactus Hill, Virginia*
19  Monte Verde, Chile

*dates are not accepted by all archaeologists

## Clovis Sites, or Sites Less than 13,500 Years
(these sites contain Clovis points)

5   Anzick, Montana
6   East Wenatchee, Washington
7   Lange-Ferguson, South Dakota
9   Paleo Crossing, Ohio
11  Shawnee Minisink, Pennsylvania
13  Arlington Springs, California
14  Lehner, Arizona
15  Clovis, New Mexcio
16  Aubrey, Texas
17  Sloth Hole, Florida

## Clovis Age Sites, or Sites Less Than 13,500 Years
(South American sites do not contain Clovis points)

18  Quebrada Santa Julia, Chile
20  Cerro Tres Tetas, Argentina and Cueva Casa del Minero, Argentina
21  Piedra Museo, Argentina
22  Fell's Cave, Chile

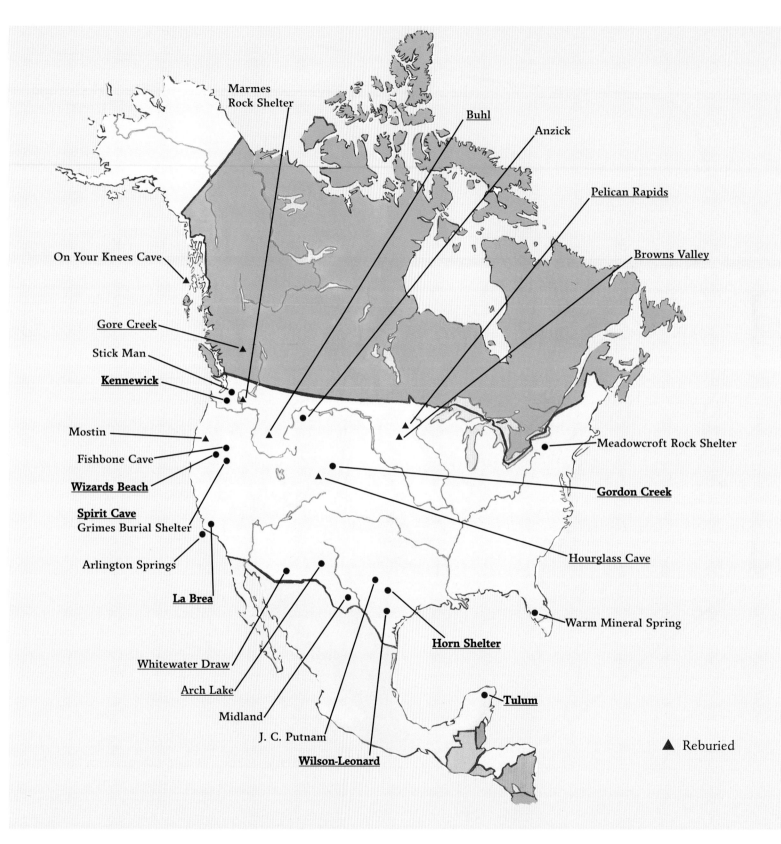

Marmes
Rock Shelter

Buhl

Anzick

Pelican Rapids

Browns Valley

On Your Knees Cave

Gore Creek

Stick Man

**Kennewick**

Mostin

Fishbone Cave

**Wizards Beach**

**Spirit Cave**
Grimes Burial Shelter

Arlington Springs

**La Brea**

Meadowcroft Rock Shelter

**Gordon Creek**

Hourglass Cave

Warm Mineral Spring

**Horn Shelter**

Whitewater Draw

Arch Lake

Midland

J. C. Putnam

**Wilson-Leonard**

**Tulum**

▲ Reburied

## Ancient Skeletons of North America

About forty human remains dating from 9,000 years ago or earlier have been reported in North America. This figure includes remains where only several bones were found. Some of the sites listed represent more than one skeleton. <u>Underlined</u> names indicate sites for skeletons that have at least half of their bones. **Boldface** names indicate sites for skeletons that have nearly complete skulls. Kennewick Man is rare, not only for his age but because his skull is in good condition and his set of bones is nearly intact. This is one reason the issue of his repatriation has caused so much interest within the scientific community. Note the number of remains that have been reburied.

leaf-shaped knives. They fashioned these tools by striking round river rocks and splitting them into pieces, or flakes. Then they used an antler or bone tool to shape the flakes into points or knives.

The Old Cordilleran tools also included hooks and harpoon barbs for fishing. In addition to game, the people ate large minnows, salmon, and freshwater mussels. Often they left behind big trash piles of empty shells.

Unlike the earlier people, the Old Cordilleran used the same tools and weapons wherever they traveled. Their tools were fewer and more general-purpose than those of the Western Stemmed folk. Both groups likely had atlatls, or throwing sticks. But the Old Cordilleran hunting technology was superior in at least one important way. By studying broken spear points, archaeologists have noticed that the Old Cordilleran people must have thrown their darts with great force. The darts may have had feathers. Feathered darts fly straighter. Darts that fly straight can be made from lighter materials. The end result is a faster, more accurate weapon, one that could have helped the Old Cordilleran hunters pursue small, fast-moving prey. Smaller animals make smaller targets, and so they're often harder to kill than larger ones.

The Old Cordilleran probably boiled the fish and other provisions. Water was heated with rocks that had first been put into a fire. Small burnt rocks have been found in clusters, as if they were dumped after being used for cooking. Grinding stones indicate that this group also pounded plant materials for food. Though boiling appears to have been the most common form of cooking, these people also had roasting pits and earth ovens to make plant foods edible.

Partial skeletons found at Old Cordilleran sites have

## In Kennewick Man's Time

By the time Kennewick Man/the Ancient One was born over 9,000 years ago, Ice Age glaciers had long since receded and the landscape of the Columbia Plateau had taken on its familiar modern form. Rivers and streams flow through this semiarid landscape of sagebrush, grass, scattered pine groves (and now, cultivated farmland where wheat and potatoes are grown). To the west, the Cascades rise, separating the plateau from the Pacific coast. To the east, the Rockies divide the region from the Great Plains.

On this terrain of vast grasslands, Kennewick Man likely hunted deer and perhaps also giant species of elk and bison. Like other hunter-gatherers, Kennewick Man's people camped in the lowlands in winter, near waterways. It wasn't until nearly six thousand years after Kennewick Man lived that tribes established permanent winter villages.

In the warmer months, the Ancient One may have fished for salmon. In the spring, summer, and fall, Kennewick Man's people likely followed game to higher ground. When the Ancient One climbed the foothills of the Cascades to gather plants as well as to hunt, he viewed steep, rocky, snow-covered mountains. In his era, the mountains had not yet become densely forested.

Stone spear points, atlatl (spear-thrower) hooks, bolas (stone balls), harpoon points, and other tools and weapons found in the Columbia River Basin date to Kennewick Man's time. They show how the Ancient One's people likely hunted. (*See* "Kennewick Man's Tool Kit" sidebar.) Small bone needles indicate that his people sewed their clothes. Like those who came after them, they may have worn garments of tanned buckskin.

Woven baskets and bags dating from the Ancient One's time have been found in sites on the Great Basin, the region south of the Columbia Plateau. Like the ancient people of the Great Basin, Kennewick Man's people probably twined cords and rope, and made coiled baskets from Indian hemp, bunchgrass, and other plants. The twined mats encasing the 9,400-year-old partially mummified man found in Nevada and known as the Spirit Cave Mummy show the great skill of ancient artisans. The mummy was found wearing a cloak of rabbit fur that had been twined into strips. (*See* "The Spirit Cave Mummy" sidebar.) Possibly Kennewick Man's people also wore cloaks—twined either from plants such as Indian hemp or from the fur of animals such as rabbits or wolves.

In a cave in Fort Rock, Oregon, archaeologists unearthed a cache of seventy-five rope sandals dating from approximately 9,000 to 10,000 years ago. Each twined sandal has a flat sole, a mostly enclosed front panel (open at the toes), and a tie system involving a series of interlocking loops fixed to one edge of the sole. Using tough fibers like sagebrush and bunchgrass, readily available to them on the

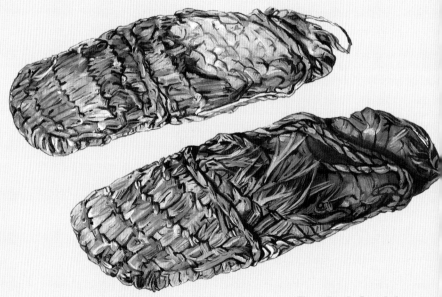

*Fort Rock Sandals*

Columbia Plateau, the Ancient One's folk might well have made themselves such rope sandals.

Kennewick Man's people may have traded with coastal groups. Olivella shell beads from the Marmes Rockshelter in eastern Washington, not far from Kennewick, indicate such trade. Or ancient Columbia Plateau people may have journeyed hundreds of miles west across the Cascade Range to the Pacific.

Paleoindians, perhaps as far back as Kennewick Man's time, left many pictographs etched into and painted on rocks. Pictographs found along the Mid-Columbia and Lower Snake rivers show humanlike figures with arcs above their heads and projecting rays. Though no one knows for sure, the pictographs seem connected with a belief in spirit beings.

Paleoindians of Kennewick Man's time buried their dead, sometimes first smearing them with red ocher. Some mourners left grave offerings such as spear points, beaded necklaces, and bone needles. A bear-tooth pendant and an owl's foot wrapped in stone flakes, both found at the Marmes Rockshelter (but not with human remains), suggest rituals were part of their lives.

Some of the ancient people cremated their dead. In at least a few cases, they cut the flesh off the bones, perhaps as a ritual, for easier transport, or to allow the bones to burn faster.

The remains of about forty individuals 9,000 years or older have been discovered in North America. These include incomplete skeletons consisting of only a few bones. From this relatively small group, the data suggest that men lived to be thirty-two to forty years old on average. Women, on average, died between the ages of eighteen and twenty-three. Only two skeletons of women over twenty-five

years old have been found. It's possible that many young women died from complications of childbirth, and that many children died before reaching adulthood. Eight of the remains found were of children, ranging from one-and-a-half to thirteen years of age.

The small sampling indicates that men generally grew to a height averaging five feet, six inches. Some, like Kennewick Man, developed powerful muscles, while others were less robust. The women (as four nearly complete skeletons indicate) stopped growing at around five feet.

Lines in the bones and in the enamel of the teeth of child and adolescent skeletons show that these ancient people experienced times of hunger, often on a yearly basis, and probably in winter. The 12,400-year-old skeleton of a young woman now known as Buhl Woman, found in Idaho, is just such a case. The teeth of half the individuals, both adults and adolescents, show interruptions in tooth growth, especially between the ages of two and a half and five. Women probably stopped giving their children milk between those years and gave birth about every four years.

It seems that the ancient hunter-gatherers had violent lifestyles. Eight out of ten male skeletons complete enough to study show evidence of major injuries. The nature of some of these injuries suggests wounds inflicted by other people (as opposed to wounds received accidentally, such as during a hunt). It appears that assailants stabbed both Kennewick Man and a middle-aged man found at the Grimes Burial Shelter in Nevada. The Spirit Cave Mummy and three individuals found in Washington State—Stick Man, Kennewick Man, and a male skeleton found at the Marmes Rockshelter—all suffered skull fractures. None of the female skeletons show evidence of violent injuries.

*A Cascade point, perhaps similar to the one found in Kennewick Man's pelvis*

many cavities and missing teeth. However, teeth that remain show very little wear. This indicates that these later people consumed soft foods made from plants—perhaps porridges. Such foods contained natural sugars, which caused cavities. The minimal wear on the teeth suggests that the peoples' food was well cooked when they ate it.

Few remains exist of the dwellings of Western Stemmed people. They often used natural rock shelters. Remains of one small semicircular shelter, perhaps little more than a wind break or small skin tent, have been found in Oregon. Patterns in the soil at some Old Cordilleran sites seem to indicate that the group sometimes lived in small, domed dwellings and at other times lived in dwellings that were partially underground.

Burials at six Old Cordilleran sites, all of which contained more than one individual, have been discovered on the Columbia Plateau. The sites indicate that the Old Cordilleran people buried their dead. The Western Stemmed people may have had a practice of burying their dead, but there is little physical evidence for this. At two Western Stemmed sites, archaeologists have found cremated remains. Ancient people sometimes cremated bodies in order to transport the dead more easily. At times, especially because the groups moved frequently, a loved one may have died far away from a desired final resting place.

Archaeological discoveries show that within two thousand years of Kennewick Man's death, the Western Stemmed Tradition had vanished. Why did the Old Cordilleran way of life become the way of the future? Environmental changes likely relate to the changes in lifestyles, yet many questions remain unanswered.

Were the two groups distinct ethnic populations who may have crossed the Bering Land Bridge at different times? If so, did the earlier group die out, or intermarry and merge with the later? Or were the groups the same population following varying traditions? And to which tradition did Kennewick Man belong?

If looking at dates, and perhaps the wear patterns on the Ancient One's teeth, archaeologists might place him in the Western Stemmed Tradition. But if Kennewick Man belongs to the earlier group, one curious fact cannot be explained. The leaf-shaped projectile point embedded in his pelvis is of a style associated with the Old Cordilleran Tradition. This type is now known as a Cascade point. Though it appears in Columbia Plateau sites dating from after 9,000 years ago, the Cascade point is not known there from sites lived in as early as Kennewick Man's time.

In his book *Ancient Encounters*, Chatters envisions the groups to be two distinct populations, and he imagines a dramatic scene as a way to explain how Kennewick Man received his hip wound. There's a scarcity of women in both groups, and in a violent encounter, the Ancient One fights to try to prevent another man from stealing his female companion.

Of course, it cannot be known whether the Old Cordilleran and the Western Stemmed were two populations or that they fought with one another. If so, they might have fought over food. Or perhaps a member of Kennewick Man's own group struck him. Or he could have been wounded in a hunting accident. A number of intriguing scenarios can be created. Yet not all archaeological puzzles can be solved, or mysteries explained.

The research relating to Kennewick Man, like all studies in the field of archaeology, offers clues and insights. Together, many clues add understanding of humankind—who we are, as well as how we came to be.

## Kennewick Man's Tool Kit

No tools were found buried with Kennewick Man, so we cannot know for sure what tools he used or what they looked like. But based on objects found at sites of the same time period, we can make an educated guess.

The collection of sharpened stone tools that Kennewick Man no doubt carried with him served many purposes. He would have used them to kill, skin, and butcher deer and other animals. As he ate, he may have held a stone knife to cut the meat into smaller chunks.

Kennewick Man likely fashioned blades in a variety of shapes and sizes, following a method he'd learned from his father or other adults. Using a larger stone, or perhaps a deer antler, he'd chip off small flakes from a stone, blow by blow, until satisfied with the result. It took skill to make blades and spear points like the ones on the next pages. Over the years, Kennewick Man probably discarded many tools that didn't turn out exactly the way he wanted. He would have regularly resharpened and repaired his tools. His survival and the survival of others in his band depended on his success as a hunter, and that success depended on the tools he used.

For their tools, prehistoric people preferred certain kinds of stones, such as obsidian (volcanic glass) and agate, because they were strong but broke in a predictable way when struck. There is no obsidian on the Columbia Plateau, but there was a stone called chalcedony.

Kennewick Man would have hafted, or fitted, his points to shafts or foreshafts with sinew or twine. Kennewick Man's strip of sinew would likely have come from a buck, or male deer. He may have also used a glue (made from animal fat, tree resin, and blood) to further lock his spear points in place.

Here are tools and weapons Kennewick Man could have carried with him, perhaps inside a shoulder bag:

**1.** a lump of red ocher, which may have been used for making designs on bodies or rocks, for decorating deceased loved ones before burial, or as an insect repellant

**2.** a crescent (fragment shown here; archaeologists do not know the purpose of this tool)

**3. a)** and **b)** scrapers for shaping bone and wood

**4.** a bone needle for sewing

**5.** a bola—a set of stones tied together, used to stun and snare birds and long-legged animals

**6. a) b) c) d)** spear points for killing game animals (and also sometimes employed as knives for cutting); one point **(e)** is hafted to a foreshaft with sinew, or animal tendon

**7.** a barbed harpoon point, possibly for spearing fish; Kennewick Man may have fastened it to the same foreshaft he used for his spear points.

The foreshaft (the piece that holds the spear point) would have been attached to a spear shaft. The spear shaft likely fit into an atlatl, or throwing stick. These items have not been illustrated because there are no surviving examples of them from Kennewick Man's time period. The tool kit may have also included a roll of hemp twine for tying things together. Butchering was probably done with flakes, or sharp-edged pieces broken off from rocks.

**1**

**2**

**3a**

**3b**

**4**

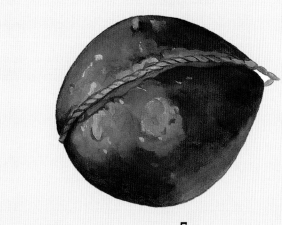

**5**

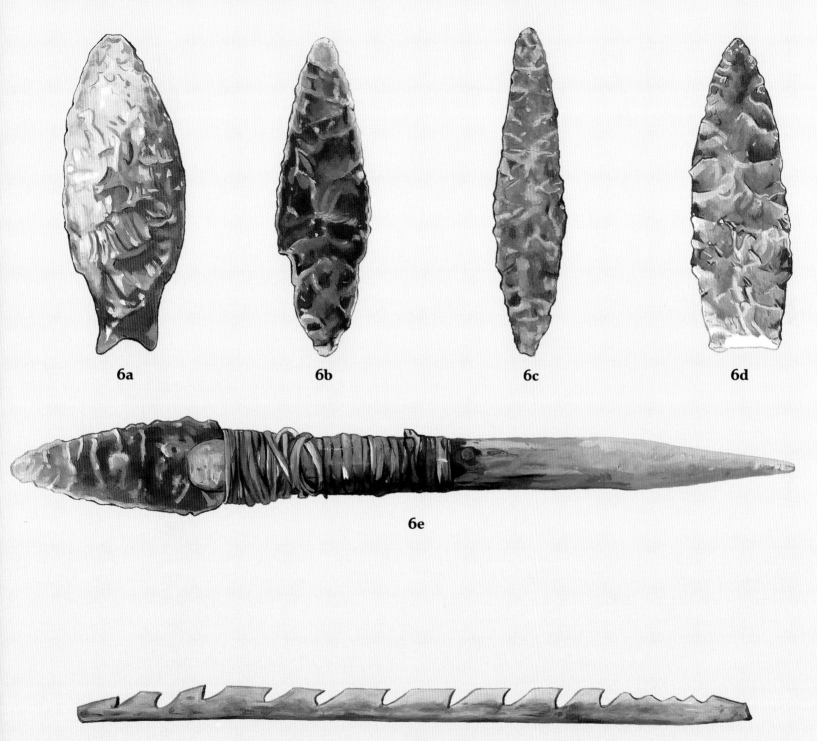

6a 6b 6c 6d

6e

7

# The Future for Kennewick Man and Other Skeletons

Kennewick Man continues to stay in special protective storage at the Burke Museum in Seattle. It's possible that eventually the Army Corps of Engineers will transfer the bones to another place for safekeeping, such as one of the major tribal museums in the Pacific Northwest. Or if there are future legal decisions made by federal agencies or Congress, Kennewick Man could be repatriated by one or more Native American tribes.

The debates over why the skeleton looks different from those of modern-day Native Americans continue. Studies of skull shapes have taught physical anthropologists much—in fact, a large part of the history of evolution has been based on skull shapes. However, such studies offer limited information. If scientists ever retrieve DNA from Kennewick Man, there may yet be important new information about the biological makeup of early North Americans.

The tribes continue to talk with the Army Corps of Engineers to do what they can to protect the Ancient One from further destructive testing. New genetic tests require ever-smaller bits of material to achieve results, and it's possible that someday DNA could be extracted from the bone fragments already sampled from the skeleton. Until new technological processes are developed, it's unclear whether the Corps will allow Kennewick Man to undergo any additional examinations or tests.

Meanwhile, every six months Kennewick Man undergoes a checkup. Curators at the Burke Museum download data from a small computer that records the temperature and humidity inside the storage locker. Handling the bones as little as possible, the curators open each case to see that no damage has occurred since the last inspection. Should a new crack appear, the curators would record the change and stabilize the bone if necessary by wrapping its pieces to keep them together. Sometimes during these checks, scientists or tribal members are allowed to be present.

Though the claimant tribes were profoundly disappointed by the results of the suit, some members acknowledge that despite—or maybe even *because of*—this setback involving the Ancient One, the tribes have made great strides in repatriating many other ancestors. Also, the regular contact with one another has helped the tribes develop cooperative working relationships. Joined by another native tribe, the Confederated Tribes of Warm Springs, the coalition sped up and simplified the process of filing other NAGPRA claims. Since the conclusion of the Ancient One trial, the tribes have repatriated the remains of hundreds of individuals and thousands of burial artifacts from fourteen different museums, universities, and federal agencies.

In June 2007, five years after Judge Jelderks's decision, representatives from the tribes gathered at the Burke Museum for one of the biggest repatriations since the passing of NAGPRA in 1990. The transfer took place in two installments, six months apart. The bones of at least 180

## On Your Knees Cave: A Successful Collaboration

In the case of a 9,200-year-old partial human skeleton, found on Prince of Wales Island, off Ketchikan, Alaska, in July 1996, archaeologists and native peoples formed an amicable working relationship. Immediately upon discovery of a human jawbone, pelvic bone, and bone fragments in On Your Knees Cave, the U.S. Forest Service contacted the local tribes. Brought together under the mandate of NAGPRA, two Tlingit communities and archaeologists from the Tongass National Forest took part in a series of discussions that led to a respectful written agreement between the parties.

The Forest Service agreed to discuss all decisions relating to the excavation with the Tlingit. Though it was within their rights under NAGPRA to refuse testing, the native peoples agreed to allow radiocarbon dating and DNA testing of the bones. They gave permission for the tests with the understanding that the bones would later be reburied in the cave. The archaeologists agreed to notify the tribe of any news before telling others. Young tribal members took part in the excavation as paid interns. During the several years in which the excavation took place, archaeologists participated in native ceremonies.

The bones were found to be of a young man, probably in his twenties. The cave had been a bear's den. The human bones could have been dragged into the cave by bears. Isotope studies involving the chemical elements of the bones revealed that the ancient man ate fish and sea mammals such as seals. Scientists succeeded in extracting usable DNA from a tooth and learned that the ancient man belonged to a group linked both to Native Americans and Northern Asians.

"The way we interpreted this find was that an ancestor was offering himself to us to give us knowledge," said Rosita Worl, a Tlingit tribal member and anthropologist and president of the Sealaska Heritage Institute.

The excavation at On Your Knees Cave shows that collaboration is possible between tribal nations and anthropologists. Many of the 500 federally recognized Native American tribes in the United States employ and work closely with archaeologists—including Native Americans who are also archaeologists. Some Native Americans are willing to bend on the issue of allowing human remains to be studied. Likewise, most archaeologists are willing to compromise on the issue of reburying the dead. How different might the Kennewick Man case have been had both the native groups and the scientists been willing to make such concessions?

individuals and 21,660 funerary objects were involved. All came from the Columbia Plateau collections at the Burke Museum and Central Washington University. Some of the ancestral remains had been held in storage in the museum for more than a hundred years.

The process of making inventories, compiling detailed reports, filing legal paperwork, and consulting with tribal representatives took nearly a decade. At the invitation of the tribes, several museum staff members attended the reburial ceremony at a secret location somewhere in Washington or Oregon, not far from the Columbia River.

Though not undertaking litigation at this time regarding the Ancient One, the tribes remain active in their pursuit of repatriating ancient skeletons by serving on committees that seek to amend NAGPRA. Joining with other tribes across the nation, they want to see changes in the law so that the term "Native American" is more clearly defined. The difference in wording would make it easier for tribes to claim skeletons now held in museums, as well as those yet to be discovered. Several bills of this type have recently been proposed in the U.S. Senate. There have also been proposals for counterlegislation. So far, none of the bills has passed.

How the Kennewick Man ruling will affect the outcome of other suits involving NAGPRA remains to be seen. A similar case involves the Spirit Cave Mummy, the partially mummified human remains found in Spirit Cave, Nevada. It has become the focus of a dispute between the Fallon Paiute-Shoshone Tribe and the U.S. Bureau of Land Management.

NAGPRA is part of a global movement toward promoting and protecting the rights of indigenous peoples. Though most countries of the world do not have legislation equivalent to NAGPRA, many international organizations and nongovernmental groups are assisting native peoples in issues of cultural property rights.

In the case of Kennewick Man, many factors could have influenced his story to unfold differently. Could concessions between the tribes, the government, and the scientists have been made without any of the parties going to court? The results from the Kennewick Man court case have not been all bad. Scientists have come up with some important and interesting research. And the ill feelings and legal wrangling that occurred ultimately show the need for greater awareness, respect, and cooperation among groups. Native American leaders, scientists, lawyers, and government officials are now discussing ways to move forward if and when another ancient skeleton is found; no one wants to repeat the mistakes of the past.

The story of the Ancient One/Kennewick Man has raised important moral, ethical, and legal questions. Who should determine the treatment of ancient human remains? What are the potential benefits of knowledge and education in relation to these remains? Do these benefits outweigh considerations for respecting customs and traditions? What values do all people share? How can we forge a clear vision of understanding between groups of people with different backgrounds and beliefs? The issues are complex, and it will take time and much sensitivity among all parties to bring about positive solutions.

Whether he is known as Kennewick Man or the Ancient One, this prehistoric hunter-gatherer has prompted scholars to reassess humanity's origins and has raised many questions about our future.

# Glossary

**Ainu (EYE-nu)**—an ethnic group considered to be the first inhabitants of Japan. Full-blooded Ainu are mostly fair skinned, though they are not Caucasian.

**American Indian**—a general term applied to the members of aboriginal peoples living in North America and South America. "American Indian" and "Native American" are often used interchangeably, though "Native American" also includes Inuit and native Hawaiians.

**ancestor**—one from whom a person is descended and who is usually more remote in the line of descent than a grandparent.

**anthropologist**—a scientist who studies humans and their ancestors.

**anthropology**—from two Greek words meaning "study of humans." Anthropologists investigate human cultural, social, and physical development as well as human origins and behavior. Branches of anthropology include physical anthropology (the study of human origins, physical characteristics, skeletons, and genetic makeup), cultural anthropology (the study of humans through their art, language, religion, dress, habits, technology, government, and social structure), ethnology (the study of the world's people and cultures), and archaeology (the study of people and cultures of the past through artifacts).

**archaeological site**—a place or location in which evidence of past human activity is preserved.

**archaeologist**—a scientist who studies and seeks to interpret and understand humans and their cultures of the past, primarily through the recovery and analysis of materials or artifacts that have been left behind. See *artifact*.

**artifact**—an object made by humans or one, such as an antler tool, that is modified by humans.

**atlatl**—an ancient spear-throwing tool made from a wooden rod; used for warfare and hunting. The bottom end of a spear was placed in a notch at one end of the atlatl. Holding the other end, a person would hurl the rod and launch the spear. The spear traveled longer distances and moved with greater speed, force, and accuracy than a spear thrown with the arm alone. For more than 10,000 years, ancient people used atlatls until they developed bows and arrows.

**Beringia or Bering Land Bridge**—a bridge of land that is believed to have once connected Asia and North America.

**bola**—a weapon consisting of two or more stones attached to the ends of a cord. The weapon is hurled at animals to entangle them.

**carbon 14 testing**—see *radiocarbon dating*.

**Cascade point**—a kind of spear point hunter-gatherers used in the central Washington area thousands of years ago. It has a pointed base, not a flat base.

**Caucasian race (sometimes known as the Caucasoid race)**—a term of racial classification, coined around 1800, for the "white" race. It has been used to describe populations of Europe, North Africa, the Middle East, and parts of Central and South Asia. Or if the term is used more narrowly, it can refer to people of European origin, or to classify people by skin color only. Despite the advice of many scientists, this term sometimes refers to people of a certain range of physical features.

**Clovis point**—a finely crafted and distinctly large spear point fashioned by the Clovis people, who first appeared in North America around 13,500 years ago.

cobble—a naturally rounded stone, usually from a river, used to break other stones.

coprolite—fossilized feces or dung.

CT (computerized tomography) scan—a series of X-ray images taken from different angles. The multiple X-rays are then rendered in cross section in pictures by filtering them through a computer program.

defendant—a person who is being accused in a legal action.

DNA (deoxyribonucleic acid)—the substance that carries genetic information in the cells of animals and plants.

ethnic replacement—when a human population becomes extinct and is replaced by another human population. This process may occur randomly, as one group dies out from natural causes, or can occur when groups fight with one another, as in competing over territory or resources. (See *extinct*.)

evolution—process of change in living things. In biological terms, it is the change in the genetic material of a population of organisms over many generations.

extinct—no longer in existence.

Federal land—land owned by the government.

Federal magistrate—a government judge.

flake—a piece or chip from a stone tool or point.

flint—a term usually referring to a kind of hard dark quartz used to fashion tools or to start a fire. The term originated in England, where it refers specifically to chert, another variety of rock that can

be easily broken to form sharp points.

flint knapping—see *knapping*.

forensics—the scientific study of physical evidence.

foreshaft—a small secondary shaft that is inserted into the hunter's mainshaft. Ancient hunters probably carried at least one mainshaft and multiple foreshafts, each foreshaft hafted with a different point or barbed harpoon. The foreshaft enabled hunters to change a broken stone point, or "load" a different point when desired, according to the hunting circumstance.

fossil—the remains of an ancient living thing that has become preserved in rock.

genetics—a branch of biology that deals with the heredity and variation among living things.

geologist—a scientist who studies the history of the earth through rocks and stones.

glacier—a large body of ice moving slowly down a slope or valley.

Great Basin—a mostly arid region between the Sierra Nevada and Wasatch mountains in the western United States. It includes most of Nevada and parts of California, Idaho, Utah, Wyoming, and Oregon.

Great Plains—a broad expanse of grasslands and prairie which lies west of the Mississippi River and east of the Rocky Mountains in the United States and Canada. This area includes parts of Colorado, Kansas, Montana, Nebraska, New Mexico, North Dakota, Oklahoma, South

Dakota, Texas, Wyoming, and the Canadian provinces of Alberta, Manitoba, and Saskatchewan.

hammer stone—a cobble that fits into the hand, usually oval in shape, used to strike other stones in order to make tools. (See *knapping*.)

haplogroup—a pattern of genetic markers passed unchanged through generations of humans. Haplogroups are defined by specific DNA patterns. Haplogroups can be used to trace back to a common ancestor of two different groups of present-day people. (See *DNA*.)

hunter-gatherers—people who obtain their food by hunting animals, fishing, and gathering plants. Hunter-gatherers are not farmers and do not raise domestic animals for food.

Ice Age—an ice age is a long period of cold climate when glaciers may form over large areas of land. In the last 500 million years, there have been four great ice ages. The last one is often called the Ice Age. It occurred at the end of the Pleistocene Epoch, a geologic time period between 1.8 million and 11,500 years ago.

isotope study—a technique for understanding the chemical composition of a substance that involves identifying chemical elements according to their atomic mass (such as helium-3 and carbon-13). Through isotope study, scientists can determine which elements, and how much of certain elements, are contained in a sample.

knapping—a method of shaping stone by

breaking off small chips or flakes with quick blows from a hammer stone or antler.

**lithic**—relating to an artifact or tool made of stone.

**migration**—the process of moving from one place or location to another.

**Native American Graves Protection and Repatriation Act (NAGPRA)**—a law which protects Native American graves and provides guidelines for custodianship of native remains and burial objects.

**obsidian**—a glass-like, volcanic rock often used by the peoples of the Pacific Northwest for spear points because it breaks in predictable ways and can make sharp edges.

**Paleoindian**—early hunter-gathering people of the Americas.

**paleontology**—the study of ancient life through fossils.

**physical anthropology (or biological anthropology)**—see *anthropology*.

**plaintiff**—a person who sues in a legal action or suit.

**plateau**—a land area that has a generally level surface. In the context of this book, the Columbia Plateau refers to a specific area located in parts of western Canada, Washington, Oregon, Idaho, and Montana that includes hills, mountains, and canyons, as well as flat land.

**prehistoric**—the period before the invention of writing. The prehistoric era in North America differs from the prehistoric era in other parts of the world where writing came thousands of years earlier.

**race**—usually refers to a group of people who share certain physical traits, interests, origins, or characteristics. It is a social term, used to distinguish groups from one another; it is not a scientific term based on biology.

**radiocarbon dating**—a technique used to calculate an object's age. All living things, including animals and plants, absorb the element carbon, or C-14. When the living thing dies, the absorbed carbon starts to break down. Scientists can tell the age of the object based on how much carbon 14 it still holds.

**refuse pit**—large hole in the ground used for garbage.

**repatriation**—to return to a place or country of origin.

**reservation**—land set aside for a particular use, such as the relocation of Native Americans in the 1800s. In the context of this book, it is an area of land managed by a Native American tribe under the United States Department of the Interior's Bureau of Indian Affairs. There are about 310 Indian reservations in the United States.

**rock shelter**—a small cave or shallow opening at the base of an overhanging slab of rock or cliff.

**scraper**—stone tool used for scraping animal hides. It was worked, or sharpened, only along one edge, so the tool could be held in the palm of the hand without injuring the person who was using it. One of the types of scrapers most commonly found from Kennewick Man's time period was the "side scraper." It was made from a rectangular stone that was worked, or crafted, on the longest side.

**sinew**—animal tendon, which prehistoric humans used for cords or thread.

**skeleton**—the rigid supportive or protective structure or framework of an organism.

**skull**—a skeleton head that includes the brain case, face, and lower jaw (called the mandible).

**spear point**—a sharpened piece of stone attached to the end of a spear or the sharpened end of a spear.

**tribe**—a social group made up of numerous families. In the context of this book, tribe refers to a distinct Native American group that has survived as an intact political community.

# Time Line

**November 16, 1990**—The Native American Graves Protection and Repatriation Act (NAGPRA) is signed into law by President George H. W. Bush.

**July 28, 1996**—Kennewick Man/the Ancient One's skull is found in the Columbia River near Kennewick, Washington. The coroner gives the skull to local archaeologist Jim Chatters to determine its approximate age and ethnicity. (Chatters finds more bones from July 28 to August 29).

**July 29 and 30, 1996**—The bones are X-rayed and CT-scanned. The U.S. Army Corps of Engineers is informed of the discovery. The Corps contacts the Confederated Tribes of the Umatilla Indian Reservation.

**August 5, 1996**—A tiny bone is sent to the University of California, Riverside, for radiocarbon testing. Afterward, it is sent on to the University of California, Davis, for DNA testing.

**August 26, 1996**—The lab at the University of California, Riverside, reports that the bone is 9,330-9,580 years old (8,410 radiocarbon years).

**August 27, 1996**—After a press conference at the Kennewick City Hall, the public becomes aware of the skeleton's age.

**August 30, 1996**—The Benton County coroner collects the bones from Jim Chatters and takes them to the local sheriff's office.

**September 2, 1996**—The Army Corps of Engineers takes control of the bones and moves them to a more secure facility.

**September 9, 1996**—The Confederated Tribes of the Umatilla Indian Reservation, the Confederated Tribes of the Colville Reservation, the Nez Percé Tribe, the Wanapum Band, and Confederated Tribes and Bands of the Yakama Nation jointly claim the human remains under NAGPRA.

**September 17, 1996**—The Army Corps of Engineers agrees to the joint tribal claim and releases an official "Notice of Intent to Repatriate" statement.

**October 16, 1996**—Eight anthropologists collectively known as *Bonnichsen et al* file suit in the U.S. District Court in Portland, Oregon, to prevent the Army Corps of Engineers from repatriating the remains to the tribes and to allow further study of the remains.

**October 24, 1996**—Litigation begins in the U.S. District Court.

**April 1, 1998**—The Army Corps of Engineers transfers control of Kennewick Man to the U.S. Department of the Interior, which agrees to assist the Corps in resolving the issues related to the Federal court concerning the skeleton.

**June 17, 1998**—Out-of-court mediation begins.

October 29, 1998—Kennewick Man's bones are moved to the Burke Museum of Natural History and Culture in Seattle.

December 11, 1998—An inventory compiled by the Army Corps of Engineers reports that bones originally part of the skeleton in 1996 are missing from Kennewick Man.

February 27, 1999—A team of anthropologists hired by the Department of the Interior presents its preliminary findings based on nondestructive examinations of the skeleton carried out at the Burke Museum.

July 27, 1999—Despite tribal opposition, the Department of the Interior announces its decision to conduct destructive testing of Kennewick Man's skeleton in order to confirm the age of the bones.

January 12, 2000—Radiocarbon dating confirms that Kennewick Man is about 9,300–9,500 years old.

September 24, 2000—The Department of the Interior announces that the skeleton is Native American and rules that the bones be given to the claimant tribes.

June 22, 2001—The missing Kennewick Man bones are found; the FBI concludes its investigation but makes no arrests.

August 30, 2002—Judge John Jelderks in Portland rules that the Army Corps of Engineers must make the bones available for study. His ruling states that because Kennewick Man cannot be linked to any modern tribal group, he was not Native American as defined by NAGPRA. Jelderks therefore finds that NAGPRA does not apply in this case.

October 28, 2002—Four of the five claimant tribes file notice that they will appeal the ruling rejecting their request to bury the skeleton.

February 4, 2004—The U.S. Court of Appeals for the Ninth Circuit unanimously upholds Jelderks's ruling.

July 22, 2004—The Justice Department and tribal coalition decide they won't appeal the *Bonnichsen et al* decision to the U.S. Supreme Court.

January and February, 2006—The plaintiff scientists and their teams study Kennewick Man.

2006–present—While awaiting instructions from the Army Corps of Engineers, the Burke Museum continues to provide a secure repository for Kennewick Man/the Ancient One.

# Selected Bibliography

## Books for Young Readers

Adams, Bradley J. *Forensic Anthropology*. New York: Chelsea House, 2007.

Aveni, Anthony F. *The First Americans: The Story of Where They Came from and Who They Became*. New York: Scholastic, 2005.

Lauber, Patricia. *Who Came First? New Clues to Prehistoric Americans*. Washington, D.C.: National Geographic, 2003.

Meltzer, David J. *Search for the First Americans*. Washington, D.C.: Smithsonian Institution, 1993.

Parker, Steve. *Eyewitness Books: Skeleton*. New York: Alfred A. Knopf, 1988.

## Reference Books

Adovasio, J. M., with Jake Page. *The First Americans: In Pursuit of Archaeology's Greatest Mystery*. New York: Random House, 2002.

Benedict, Jeff. *No Bone Unturned: The Adventures of a Top Smithsonian Forensic Scientist and the Legal Battle for America's Oldest Skeletons*. New York: HarperCollins, 2003.

Burke, Heather, and Claire Smith, Dorothy Lippert, Joe Watkins, and Larry Zimmerman, eds. *Kennewick Man: Perspectives on the Ancient One*. Walnut Creek, CA: Left Coast Press, 2008.

Chatters, James C. *Ancient Encounters: Kennewick Man and the First Americans*. New York: Simon & Schuster, 2001.

Dillehay, Tom. *The Settlement of the Americas: A New Prehistory*. New York: Basic Books, 2000.

Downey, Roger. *Riddle of the Bones: Politics, Science, Race, and the Story of Kennewick Man*. New York: Copernicus, 2000.

*Handbook of North American Indians, Vol. 12, Plateau*. Edited by Deward E. Walker, Jr. Smithsonian Institution, Washington, D.C.: Government Printing Office, 1998.

Jablonski, Nina G., ed. *The First Americans: The Pleistocene Colonization of the New World*. San Francisco: California Academy of Sciences, 2002.

Karson, Jennifer, ed. *Wiyáxayxt/Wiyáaka awn = As days go by: our history, our land, and our people–the Cayuse, Umatilla, and Walla Walla*. Pendleton, Tamástslikt Cultural Institute; Portland: Oregon Historical Society; Seattle: distributed by the University of Washington Press, 2006.

Kirk, Ruth, and Richard D. Daugherty. *Archaeology in Washington*, rev. ed. Seattle: University of Washington Press, 2007.

Koppel, Tom. *Lost World: Rewriting Prehistory–How New Science Is Tracing America's Ice Age Mariners*. New York: Atria Books, 2003.

Meltzer, David J. *First Peoples in a New World: Colonizing Ice Age America*. Berkeley, CA: University of California Press, 2009.

Mihesuah, Devon A., ed. *Repatriation Reader: Who Owns American Indian Remains?* Lincoln, NE: University of Nebraska Press, 2000.

Powell, Joseph F. *The First Americans: Race, Evolution, and the Origin of Native Americans*. New York: Cambridge University Press, 2005.

Ruby, Robert H., and John A. Brown. *Indians of the Pacific Northwest: A History*. Norman, OK: University of Oklahoma Press, 1981.

Stewart, Hilary. *Stone, Bone, Antler & Shell: Artifacts of the Northwest Coast*. Seattle: University of Washington Press, 1973.

Taylor, Karen T. *Forensic Art and Illustration*. Boca Raton, FL: CRC Press, 2001.

Thomas, David Hurst. *Skull Wars: Kennewick Man, Archaeology, and the Battle for Native American Identity*. New York: Basic Books, 2000.

Watkins, Joe. *Indigenous Archaeology: American Indian Values and Scientific Practice*. Walnut Creek, CA: Alta Mira Press, 2000.

## Articles

Dansie, Amy, et al. Articles about the Spirit Cave Mummy in *Nevada State Quarterly* 40 (Spring 1997): 1-153.

Goebel, Ted, Michael R. Waters, and Dennis H. O'Rourke, "The Late Pleistocene Dispersal of Modern Humans in the Americas." *Science* 319 (March 14, 2008): 1497-1502.

Hitt, Jack. "Mighty White of You: Racial Preferences Color America's Oldest Skulls and Bones." *Harper's* (July 2005): 39-55.

Kluger, Jeffery. "Who Should Own the Bones?" *Time* (March 13, 2006): 50-51.

Lemonick, Michael D., and Andrea Dorfman. "Who Were the First Americans?" *Time* (March 13, 2006): 44-52.

Parfit, Michael. "Hunt for the First Americans." *National Geographic* (December 2000): 40-69.

Preston, Douglas. "The Lost Man." *New Yorker* (June 16, 1997): 70.

Preston, Douglas. "Skin & Bones." *New Yorker* (February 9, 1998): 52.

Rigsby, Bruce. "The Stevens Treaties, Indian Claims Commission Docket 264, and the Ancient One Known as Kennewick Man." In *The Power of Promises: Rethinking Indian Treaties in the Pacific Northwest*, edited by Alexandra Harmon, 244-75. Seattle: University of Washington Press, 2008.

Steele, D. Gentry, and Joseph F. Powell. "Facing the Past: A View of the North American Human Fossil Record." In *The First Americans: The Pleistocene Colonization of the New World*, edited by Nina G. Jablonski, 93-121, San Francisco: California Academy of Sciences, 2002.

## Websites

About.com: Archaeology
www.archaeology.about.com/od/kennewickman

Burke Museum of Natural History and Culture
www.washington.edu/burkemuseum/kman

Confederated Tribes of the Umatilla Indian Reservation
www.umatilla.nsn.us/ancient.html

Friends of America's Past
www.friendsofpast.org

HistoryLink.org
www.historylink.org

Katherine Kirkpatrick
www.katherinekirkpatrick.com

Kennewick Man Virtual Interpretive Center
www.tri-cityherald.com/kman

National Park Service
www.nps.gov/archeology/kennewick/
www.cr.nps.gov/nagpra

NOVA
www.pbs.org/wgbh/nova/first

## Documentary Films

Burke Museum of Natural History and Culture. *Kennewick Man on Trial*, lectures from the Burke Museum Symposium "Kennewick Man on Trial," February 1999. Seattle: University of Washington, October 1999.

Carver, Kyle, and Ryan Purcell. *Kennewick Man: An Epic Drama of the West*. New York: Filmmakers Library, 1997.

*NOVA*. "Mysteries of the First Americans." Boston: WGBH Public Broadcasting, 2000.

Riffe, Jed. *Who Owns the Past?* Berkeley, CA: Berkeley Media, 2002.

Sealaska Heritage Institute in collaboration with the Tongass National Forest, the Denver Museum of Nature and Science, and the National Park Service, with support from the National Science Foundation Office of Polar Programs. *Kuwóot Yas.èin: His Spirit is Looking Out from the Cave*. Juneau: Sealaska Heritage Institute, 2005.

# Research and Source Notes

*At the request of the Native American community, there are no photographs of human remains in this book.*

*See the author's website, www.katherinekirkpatrick. com, for additional sidebars, study questions, and other information.*

### Discovery

"Look over here, dude! We have a human head." Chatters, *Ancient Encounters*, 24.

"So how's Kennewick Man?" Chatters, 44.

"Are you sitting down?" Chatters, 50.

The illustration of the skeleton is adapted from art by Chatters, p. 129

### Controversy

"What's a European doing here . . . " Chatters, 64–65.

"Our old people say . . . " Minthorn, interview with the author.

"This was a man . . ." Chatters, correspondence with the author.

By 1994, physical anthropologists D. Gentry Steele and C. Loring Brace, among others, had published several scholarly articles suggesting that the earliest skeletal remains in North America differed from those of the most recent Native Americans. The publicity surrounding the discovery of Kennewick Man brought the topic to public awareness.

For statements about the Umatilla's attitude toward testing and related articles, see "Ancient One/Kennewick Man" at the Confederated Tribes of the Umatilla Indian Reservation website, www.umatilla.nsn.us/ ancient.html.

### An Ancestor or a "Find"?

For a comprehensive history of Native American grave theft, see Thomas, *Skull Wars*.

After U.S. Indian agents signed a treaty with Umatilla, Cayuse, and Walla Walla chiefs in 1855, they relocated the tribes to a single reservation in Pendleton, Oregon. The more than four million acres that the tribes ceded includes the Ancient One's discovery site in Columbia Park. The 1855 treaty, still binding today, permits the tribes to hunt, fish, and gather plants on their ceded lands. According to the treaty, the tribes also retained "other rights"—unspecified in writing but probably including the right to tend the graves of their ancestors. Kennewick Man's discovery site was traditional Walla Walla homeland, as indicated in the 1855 treaty (see Rigsby, "The Stevens Treaties").

### A Nine-Year Court Battle

On April 1, 1998, the Army Corps of Engineers transferred control of Kennewick Man, in essence the power to make certain decisions about the skeleton, to the U.S. Department of the Interior. The Department of the Interior agreed to assist the Corps in resolving issues related to the Federal court. However, the Corps retains custodianship for the actual skeleton.

In February 1999, the U.S. Department of the Interior (with the National Park Service branch) hired a team of scientists to conduct a weeklong study to determine Kennewick Man's cultural affiliation. Go to www.nps.gov/history/archeology/ kennewick/ to read their reports.

For court documents in the *Bonnichsen et al* case, go to www.friendsofpast.org/kennewick-man/ court/court.html.

### The Scientists Study the Skeleton

"Nothing was like seeing the real thing." Richard Jantz, video clip accompanying the article in "Meet Kennewick Man," *Tri-City Herald*, February 24, 2006, www.tri-cityherald.com/ kman.

### Theories and Findings

Most of the content of this chapter comes from unpublished research articles. A book by the plaintiff scientists and their teams, *Paleoamerican Origins: Beyond Clovis* (working title), will be forthcoming from Texas A&M University Press.

### The Future of Kennewick Man and Other Skeletons

For details of specific repatriations involving the Burke Museum and other institutions, see "Notices of Inventory Completions templates" on the NAGPRA website: www.nps.gov/napgra.

### What Is Race?

"Race does not exist. Racism does exist." Quotation from Charles Keyes, anthropologist, University of Washington, "Kennewick Man on Trial" traveling exhibit, Burke Museum, 2007.

The illustration of three skulls in this sidebar was inspired by a similar piece in Karen T. Taylor, *Forensic Art and Illustration*, p. 61, after an illustration by Betty Pat Gatliff.

### What is NAGPRA?

For full text of NAGPRA, see www.nps.gov/history/nagpra.

### A *Face for Kennewick Man*

The reconstructed face, as it appears in this book, is modeled after the facial bust made by James C. Chatters and artist Tom McClelland. For an alternate interpretation, see the facial reconstruction based on the recommendations of Doug Owlsley (Michael Parfit, "Hunt for the First Americans.")

### Migrations

Not everyone subscribes to the theory that the first people of North America migrated from another continent. Many Native Americans, in the Columbia Plateau and elsewhere, believe that their ancestors came into being in the geographic regions where their tribes lived for thousands of years. If their people had migrated from a different place (for example, Asia or Beringia), they say, their oral traditions would have indicated that.

The creation stories of every Columbia Plateau tribe tell of a time when mythical beings with extraordinary powers reimagined the landscape for the coming of humans. During the time of transition, the myth people took on forms such as the coyote and wolf and other animals, fish, plants, rocks, and mountains.

The oral traditions (stories passed along from one speaker to another over time) of the Columbia Plateau tribes vary slightly, but all tribes speak of their common beginning from the world of the myth people. The stories mention specific landmarks, such as Mount Saint Helens. And the geography of the Columbia Plateau is filled with mythic names and meanings. The stories also mention mammoths, Ice Age glaciers, and volcanic activity. These ties to scientifically proven, prehistoric happenings suggest that the tribes lived on the plateau for a very long time before written history.

### Ancient Skeletons of North America

The map is based on a map by Chatters, p. 192.

### Kennewick Man's Tool Kit

Because of differences in opinion as to what kind of point was found in Kennewick Man (and which points he may have owned and used), four different choices are illustrated.

The plaintiffs argued that the point in Kennewick Man's hip may have originally had a wide, flat or rounded base, one that is "Western Stemmed," known locally in the Pacific Northwest as "Windust." However, other archaeologists cite what they believe to be serrated edges on the point. Serrated edges are not found on Western Stemmed points but are typically found on Cascade points, which are oval-shaped and have a pointed, rather than a flat, base.

### On Your Knees Cave: A Successful Collaboration

"The way we interpreted this find . . ." Rosita Worl, interviewed in the film, *Kuwóot Yas.éin: His Spirit is Looking Out from the Cave*

### A Note about Dates

The dates in the "Migrations" and "Clovis Mystery" sidebars and throughout the book may differ from dates readers find in other sources. All dates here are based on tables that translate radiocarbon years (the standard measurement of time used by scientists) into ordinary calendar years. There is more than one system for making the conversion, which accounts for the inconsistency. Opinions about dates for the migrations also differ among experts.

# Acknowledgments

Thank you to all the individuals whose contributions of time, effort, and expertise made this book possible. I thank my sister, Jennifer Kirkpatrick, who shared the research journey with me and conducted interviews.

Thank you to James C. Chatters. It has been an honor and pleasure to know you and learn from you, and I appreciate the generous gift of your time on numerous occasions, as well as your reading of the manuscript, your providing references for the illustrator, and your sharing of your unpublished research papers. Thank you to my friends at the Burke Museum: Laura Phillips, Collections Manager, Archaeology, and Megon Noble, Assistant Archaeology Collections Manager; and a special thank-you to Stephanie Jolivette, Research Associate, who spent many hours reading multiple drafts, fact checking, and assisting me in various ways. Laura Phillips also made valuable comments on various drafts, gave generously of her time, and suggested several of the sidebars.

I thank D. Gentry Steele, Professor Emeritus, Department of Anthropology at Texas A&M University, for reading two drafts, talking to me about Kennewick Man, sending me articles, and leading me to other sources. I thank anthropologist Richard L. Jantz, Professor and Director, Forensic Anthropology Center, University of Tennessee, for reading a draft and sharing an unpublished research article. Sonny Trimble, Director of the Mandatory Center of Expertise for the Curation and Management of Archaeological Collections, the U.S. Army Corps of Engineers, has my thanks for reading a draft and discussing many events and issues regarding Kennewick Man.

Thank you to Jackie Cook, archaeologist, the Confederated Tribes of the Colville Reservation, for reading several drafts, teaching me much, giving generously of your time, sharing what is most important to you, and opening up a new way of thinking in me. Thank you to Armand Minthorn, the Confederated Tribes of the Umatilla Indian Reservation; it has been an honor to make your acquaintance, and I appreciate your thoughts and your involvement, and also our day together, during which you took me to the discovery site. Thank you to Roberta Hacking for crossing the mountains with me and acting as my guide through eastern Washington.

I express my thanks and gratitude to all the staff at my publisher, Holiday House. Heartfelt thanks to my editor, Julie Amper. Thank you for your hard work, patience, and insights and for being an "old fashioned" style editor, who calls me from home and always lends a listening ear. Julie, thank you for being in my life and for teaching me much over time. Special thanks to James Armstrong, the most skillful copy editor I've ever known. This book could not have happened without your keen attention to detail. I appreciate the talents and vision of Art Director Claire Counihan, and the ongoing support of Editor-in-Chief Mary Cash and Publisher John Briggs. I'm most grateful for the beautiful and very accurate artwork provided by Emma Stevenson.

As always, I appreciate the help of my writers group, Donna Bergman, Sylvie Hossack, Suzanne Williams, and others in my community of writers and friends: Meredith Berlin, Stephanie Cowell, Tonya Cunningham, David and Adele Edwards, Jayne Engle, Jane Gardner, Gail Martini-Peterson, Greta Nelson, Andrea Simon, and Sanna Stanley. I'm especially grateful for Peter Nelson's and Mary Cresse's editorial talents and suggestions and Diane Amison-Loring's excellent proofreading skills. And I am thankful for the continuing support and encouragement of my agent, Liza Pulitzer Voges.

My husband, Jonathan Tait, provided assistance in locating and explaining scientific materials. Our daughters, Gwen and Hannah, joined me in my travels and research (and by marvelous coincidence found an ancient spear point on one of our hikes).

Finally, but most important, I acknowledge the life of a man who lived a very long time ago and has taught us so much about his world, and our own—the Ancient One, Kennewick Man.

# Index